i

A Friendship, A Dime, and A Dream: The Biography of Willie Lee Buffington

Thomas K. Perry

Pocol Press

POCOL PRESS
Published in the United States of America
by Pocol Press
6023 Pocol Drive
Clifton, VA 20124
www.pocolpress.com

Publisher's Cataloguing-in-Publication

Names: Perry, Thomas K., 1952-, author.
Title: A Friendship , a dime , and a dream : the biography of Willie Lee Buffington / Thomas K. Perry
Description: Includes bibliographical references and index. | Clifton, VA: Pocol Press, 2017.
Identifiers: ISBN 978-1- 929763-70- 2 | LCCN 2016960905
Subjects: LCSH Buffington, Willie Lee. | Simpkins, Euriah. | African Americans and libraries--Southern States--History. | African Americans--Books and reading--History--20th century. | BISAC HISTORY / United States / 20th Century | POLITICAL SCIENCE / Civil Rights | SOCIAL SCIENCE / Discrimination & Race Relations
Classification: LCC Z711.9 .P47 2017 | DDC 027.47592--dc23

Library of Congress Control Number: 2016960905

Dr. Thomas F. Gossett
Teacher and Mentor

Rev. H. Michael Williams
Friend and Brother

Dr. Robert V. Williams
Hero and Librarian

Three who have made this world better
by their simple, yet courageous acts
of humanity. I am immeasurably blessed
to have known them all.

TABLE OF CONTENTS

Acknowledgements

Dr. Bob Williams, Professor Emeritus at the University of South Carolina, did much of the early work on unearthing Buffington's contributions toward ending Jim Crow segregation and providing rural African Americans in South Carolina and Georgia a chance at an education. He and Dan Lee, reference librarian at Presbyterian College, Clinton SC, answered innumerable questions and graciously gave of their time. Bob is largely responsible for working with Buffington's grandsons to contribute a substantial gathering of letters, photographs, 8 mm film, sermons, and memorabilia of their grandfather's life. This collection is now housed at the SC Library in Columbia SC.

Former students and colleagues from Paine College in Augusta GA offered personal glimpses into their relationships with the man who didn't graduate from high school until age 26, but spent most of his life as a college instructor and professor. Dr. Maurice Cherry and Dr. Mallory Millender, your gentle spirits and willingness to help in any way continue to humble me. Dr. Silas Norman and Dr. Marcus Clayton: though our conversations were shorter, thank you for those particular insights so graciously shared.

Family members and personal friends, both of Buffington and his mentor Euriah Simpkins, opened their homes and their hearts. Mary Parkman, Helen Norris and Ruby Barnes, and Rev. Arthur Holt, your recollections and insights served as more than information. They became inspirations to see this project to its completion, to tell this story of courage and friendship in such a way that it honors Willie Lee and Euriah as they so deserve.

My wife Donna, and daughter Meghan, offered encouragement and support as three cancer surgeries lengthened the time necessary to complete the research and writing. Thank you for reminding me that there is a purpose in all things, and that God brings the best from all situations in His time. My love and gratitude are always yours.

Thomas K. Perry
May 2016

Foreword

I first heard the names W.L. Buffington and the Faith Cabin Libraries movement about 20 years ago when my then graduate assistant, Ms. Robin Copp, and I were preparing three different photo exhibits relating to the history of South Carolina libraries. Robin had been doing the background work on the exhibits and I was working on the scripts for them. She brought the amazing story of Willie Lee Buffington to my attention and how his dedication to providing reading resources for black children in South Carolina through his Faith Cabin Libraries work made such a difference in their lives.

These exhibits (and the small grant the Council was able to provide to support the research) were eventually made available via the SC Humanities Council traveling exhibit program where they circulated to any interested libraries. Other writers (see bibliography in book) have followed up some parts of the story but have never told it completely.

The Faith Cabin Libraries work was the largest private, community-based movement in the Southeast (and perhaps the entire country) involved in establishing library collections for African-Americans, at a time when they were almost completely excluded from public libraries in the Southeast. Many parts of the story are both surprising and amazing. The truly amazing part was that the work was initiated by a young man who not only had his own family responsibilities but also worked full time in a textile mill.

Equally amazing was the fact that he started the work of soliciting the reading materials for the libraries with five 2-cent stamps that he mailed to churches. Later, when the first library was established in Saluda, South Carolina one of his volunteer helpers explained: "we had no books and no money: all we had was faith." The name stuck and the Faith Cabin Libraries movement became the first large-scale movement in the Southeast to provide reading materials for African-Americans. Unfortunately, our intention for more detailed work on W.L. Buffington and the Faith Cabin Libraries movement was delayed and we were never able to get back to telling the complete story. This book by Tom Perry more than makes up for our neglect these many years.

-Robert V. Williams, Distinguished Professor,
Emeritus, University of South Carolina, School of Library and
Information Science
May 2016

Introduction – The arc of the moral universe.

Walk With Him

I saw a man of another race,
Haggardly clad, and with a black face.
And turning aside with a bitter frown,
I hear an angel voice whispering down:
"Walk with him," I heard her say,
Walk only a mile along his way."
I walked with him to the highway end,
And found that man to be my friend.
With a divine Fatherhood, we're brothers,
Yet, we stood alien to each other.
Now, I hear the voice of the Master say,
In the grievous tears of a distant day:
How oft would I have gathered you…
But ye would not." O Brothers true,
How can peace on earth be wrought,
Until we learn the lessons the Master taught.

Willie Lee Buffington
August, 1926
(First year student at Martha Berry School, Rome GA)

Unlike scholarly works, this book contains sections of narrative fiction. These are the imaginary conversations between Willie Lee Buffington and Euriah Simpkins, the moments of instruction between student and teacher, the bestowing of wisdom to the younger from the older, and ultimately the sharing of love and respect between a white man and a black man during a time of suffocating segregation in the south.

But understand, this was never intended as a scholarly work. Yes, the source material is meticulously catalogued so that others who wish may further share the road in this fascinating journey toward civil rights and human dignity. But first and foremost, this book tells a story of friendship, a friendship that somehow made a difference to thousands of people who had never been able to sit and read a book, or to understand that there was a huge world out there beyond the fields and small towns. They had never been able to raise their voices in support of brave people determined to end Jim Crow law and a warped separate-but-equal mentality. And when they learned to read, when books resided close by in simple log cabin libraries they had helped to build, then that world, and that struggle, were suddenly theirs as well.

Martin Luther King Jr. noted that the arc of the moral universe is long. A nine year old boy and a 40-year old man have a chance meeting on a time-lost summer day in 1917, and words forged a bond broken only by death many years later. This is the only conversation ever recorded between the two; yet, this long journey had barely begun. Simpkins was so influential in Buffington's life and work, but no written words remain to underscore the lessons learned, the hardships foretold, or the perseverance sustained.

The poem you just read is unexpected from a young man, a sharecropper's son trapped in the same grinding poverty as his black neighbors. When his whole society tells him to hate, to assert his white privilege, he chooses the road not just less traveled, but nearly empty. These brief narratives emerged in the darndest places, completely unsummoned, and are plausible considering the available research material and the reminiscences of those who knew Buffington. Willie never forgot Euriah, insisting he be present at his ordination as a minister of the Gospel, and at his graduations from Furman University, Crozer Theological Seminary, and the University of Pennsylvania.

When Euriah Simpkins passed away in 1944, Buffington was a professor at Benedict College, a black institution in Columbia SC, and in transition to a similar position at Paine College, another minority school in Augusta GA. He followed in his mentor's footsteps, teaching for more than 30 years, forgetting neither Euriah's admonition to "be a man; the world needs men", nor his own motto "Others", that adorned the walls of every Faith Cabin Library he ever founded.

The fictional passages help tell the story, filling gaps that no amount of research ever could. They give life to the shared legacy of the two men who contributed so much, so quietly, to the movement we call civil rights. The words set the joy bells ringing, signaling good news and the possibilities of a better future to people unaccustomed to either. Willie and Euriah successfully navigated that moral arc, and left a trail for others to follow. What they may have said along the way is worth engaging the imagination and considering the implications.

Euriah Simpkins, late 1930's.
Courtesy Helen Norris and Ruby Barnes.

Willie Lee Buffington, a thoughtful young man.
Courtesy Caroliniana Library.

Chapter 1 – "The world needs men."

October 13th, 1901: Booker T. Washington accepts President Theodore Roosevelt's invitation and dines at the White House. His book, *Up From Slavery*, is published the same year.

October 16th, 1901: South Carolina Senator "Pitchfork" Ben Tillman comments on the dinner invitation, saying "The action of President Roosevelt in entertaining that nigger will necessitate our killing a thousand niggers in the South before they learn their place again."

1903: W.E.B. DuBois' most important work, *The Souls of Black Folks*, is published.

In 1908, the political star of Coleman L. Blease burned hot in his native Newberry. He had already served in both the South Carolina House of Representatives and Senate, and would soon be elected governor. Downtrodden sharecroppers and cotton mill workers found a voice in this politician whose virulent racism was legendary. Blease was the ultimate white supremacist whose platform encouraged the lynching of blacks.

December 26th, 1908: Jack Johnson wins the World Heavyweight Championship title in boxing, the first African American to do so.

That same year, not twenty miles away in Saluda, a boy was born to poor white parents, though the family did own a few hardscrabble acres of land. By age five, he worked beside his father on their failing farm, and as a teenager labored in a sawmill. Willie Lee Buffington grew up loving and supporting his black neighbors. His best friend and mentor was the teacher at the local Negro school. There wasn't a racist thought that ever found a home in the young boy's head.

Blease breathed the fire and hatred of racism into the county air, and Buffington lived to snuff it out.

Willie was born in his Grandfather Koon's house, and was two years old in August, 1910 when his mother died. He came to his Grandmother Berry's home, and brother Luther, barely four months old, headed to his Grandmother Koon's. The elder child had no recollection of his mother, but family members told the story of how he toddled after

1

an old cat one day and fell into a creek. Annie saw, and ran to snatch him from the water, preventing her little boy from drowning.

There was one book in the Berry household, the Bible, and the woman taught herself to read it by pronouncing out loud the many words she did not know. Her grandson, nicknamed Cotton Top because of his nearly white hair, soon knew the stories of David, who felled the giant Goliath with a sling and a few smooth stones; of Samuel, who heard the voice of God in the dead of night; about Jesus the Son of God, who changed everything. For three years, they were his daily companions.

"God makes the miracle, Willie Lee. When there just don't seem no way, that's the beginning of faith. There's always a miracle waiting."

Mose Buffington married Julia Annie Bodie in 1913, and the boys came back home. The next few years saw the family grow as stepsisters Annie Nelle, Nettie Mae, Winnie Idelle, Frances and Sallye filled the little cabin to overflowing. Annie Bodie never made a distinction between the two boys and the five girls she and Mose had together.

"Mrs. Buffington, how many children do you have?"

"Seven," she answered without hesitation.

It was a kindness Willie Lee never forgot. "She included my brother and me. I had the best stepmother who ever lived."[1]

1914: George Washington Carver revives the southern economy, experimenting with and finding multiple uses for the peanut.

1914: President Woodrow Wilson orders physical re-segregation of federal workplaces after almost fifty years of integrated facilities.

February 8th, 1915: The film, *The Birth of a Nation*, is released to theaters.

1915: The Ku Klux Klan is revived in Georgia.

1917: Riots in East St. Louis MO and Houston TX raise racial tension throughout the United States.

2

After Buffington's mother died, he lived in this house with his grandmother. The house is no longer standing.
Photo taken by author.

Lessons came on a regular basis for the little boy quickly assuming the responsibilities of helping tend to the family's well-being. Some of them involved learning to treat everybody decently, no matter their station in life.

"I must have been six or seven, and walking to church with my daddy and brother. On this Sunday morning I was trying to put my feet in Uncle Joe Harris' tracks going up the dusty road he had traveled earlier. I finally said something like, 'If I couldn't walk any better than Uncle Joe, I don't think I'd walk at all.'

"By this time my daddy had got me by the ear...I got jerked back to reality, and I realized that a man's age took his energy."

"I have a feeling," Daddy said, "that when you are as old as Uncle Joe you won't be walking at all."[2]

He played with the children of black sharecroppers living nearby, since they had very few white neighbors. There were no thoughts about the difference in skin color as the boys ran and played in the fields until they grew old enough to work there. Lessons about respecting people were not long in coming, and they settled deeply into the boy's mind.

"Uncle Joe was sexton of Trinity Lutheran Church, where members often gave clothes and food to him and his wife, Lucy. Born into slavery, his freedom was endorsed by his master, Billy Carson, who set aside a house and two acres of land for the couple. My grandfather made a chair for Joe, placed at the right door of the church entrance. The men entered here, while the women used the left door, and a fence ran down the middle of the sanctuary to separate the sexes. The old black man sat in that chair and listened to every sermon and lesson, and when he died he was buried in the church cemetery with no complaints from anyone."

His wife, Aunt Lucy, died some ten years later. "Gladys, a cousin of my mother, came to sing at the funeral. The hearse was there, but no one opened the door of the church, like there was some impropriety about taking Lucy inside. Someone asked if this was only going to be a graveside service, and in a strong voice that made me proud, Gladys said, 'I came to sing at Aunt Lucy's funeral, and there is no piano or organ out yonder in that cemetery.' The church doors opened up and we all went inside."[3]

The greatest lesson, though, set in motion the way the young boy lived his entire life. Cotton Top sat alone, crying. A few minutes before, in a fit of unbrotherly disdain, Luther Buffington crushed the carefully made mudpies, leaving behind an unrecognizable mess. A shadow fell across the scene, and looking up, Willie Lee saw Professor

4

Euriah Simpkins, eyes as always filled with kindness, and this time with a deep understanding of what had happened.

"Be a man, son. This world needs men."

"I hate him."

"Then you're like Cain, who hated his brother enough to kill him. No need to be like that because hatred destroys a man from the inside, sure as any sickness."

He walked on, leaving the boy to think on the words that passed between them. The boy did just that. In the coming weeks and months, Mr. Simpkins, who cut across the Buffington farm on his way to teach the children at Plum Branch Negro School, stopped and talked.

Simpkins was born in the old Edgefield District, and attended school in Graniteville. He and his wife Martha owned their home, and though they had no children of their own, they raised a half dozen whose parents struggled to make ends meet. Willie was just another recipient of their kindness.

They became friends, and Willie Lee shared his dreams of going to school, getting an education, and becoming a minister. South Carolina in the 1910's was not a place blacks and whites talked of such things together, and certainly they did not often become friends. But some deep chord was struck, and neither society nor the time, neither Jim Crow nor the Klan, could stop it.

"I spent many happy hours with the boys my age, but of your race at work, at play, hunting and fishing, and in the old swimming hole...They are very dear to my heart," he would write some years later to another black friend and mentor, Channing Tobias.[4]

Willie began attending the Centennial School when he was five, and walked three miles to the small two-room building, until he finished the seventh grade in 1919. That was not going to be good enough for Euriah Simpkins, who taught in South Carolina's public schools more than forty years and spurred many a young person to achieve goals they didn't think they could.

"I want you to get that education, become a minister, do great things. That's what men do, and the world needs men now, more than ever."

Summer and Autumn, 1919: The Red Summer occurs as race riots engulf Chicago IL, Washington DC, Knoxville TN, Indianapolis IN and Omaha NE.

5

The sundial in Buffington's back yard. It is still there.
Photo taken by author.

"Got to work with Daddy on the farm, help with the cotton planting and picking. It's the only way we survive. He can't provide for seven children all by himself. Don't you see?"

The man's faith ran deep, and with that quiet smile he offered a phrase the young boy came to know well. "God will provide, son. He always does." Secretary of his Sunday School Association for thirty years, and a Bible Class teacher in his church for his whole adult life, he was a Christian in attitude and practical living.[5]

"Grandma Berry used to say God makes the miracle, but I thought they only happened a long time ago."

The two shared a love of books, and one day the Professor lent the boy his dog-eared copy of John Bunyan's *Pilgrim's Progress*. Willie read, hungering for knowledge, for the same truths Pilgrim wanted. They had long conversations, the man encouraging the boy to do great things, the boy daring to dream.

'Soon, there will be ways to repay his kindness, to help my friends and neighbors reach for better things, too. Maybe miracles are for today as well. Just maybe.'

But harsh times settled into their small farming community, and threatened a lot more than dreams. In 1919, the Buffingtons picked twenty bales of cotton off twenty acres, receiving $.39 per pound. The next year the boll weevil infested the cotton, and off those same twenty acres the family made two bales at $.07 per pound. They lost the farm.[6]

"We worked hard, Daddy. Why this?" Cotton Top was a man at 12 years old. Mose Buffington talked to him that way.

"No fault given to anyone. Bad things happen. Good people suffer sometimes, but there's a reason for it. Somehow I think your Grandma Berry was always right about those miracles." Looking down at his eldest child, the boy so willing to work, to make things better for his family and his neighbors, the man was proud. They would need more of that pride to get through. They moved from one rented farm to another, having new surroundings almost every year.

January 1st – 7th, 1923: The Rosewood FL race riot occurs.

1923: Columbia Records signs blues artist Bessie Smith to a recording contract.

Mose found work in local sawmills for them, first in Saluda County, and then in neighboring Newberry. The father operated one of the saws, and the boy harnessed logs.

"I handled the mules, snaked the fallen logs and pulled them along, left the chain under there to get balance, pulled a lever that lifted the log across the ground to a two-wheeled log cart, and then drove to the mill."

It led to other work as well. The boy hauled lumber for Jake Culbreath, who knew the family's plight and hired him to get two loads of lumber out of his woods near home.

"I had that experience of working and being paid by a black man when I was a little fellow."[7] His brother Luther kept up the cotton patch and garden to help out the family as much as he could.

"Our neighbors were like us. We all had very little money. But we organized a Sunday School in the country schoolhouse, and every Sunday we went there in overalls. My father was the superintendent, and I began teaching classes there."[8] It may not have been the ministry as he and Euriah ultimately envisioned, but it was a start.

In time, both father and son became expert sawyers, cutting logs into rough, straight boards. Willie didn't think much about school anymore, but he was still learning hard lessons, and posing even harder questions to his elders. There was a conversation with the minister at Trinity Lutheran Church, where Uncle Joe and Aunt Lucy were buried.

"When we are saw milling and in the woods, we make coffee in a tin cup. Black folks and white folks get coffee out of that cup, drink it together. Why can't you do that at home, or at a restaurant?"

The man looked down for a long time before answering this boy who was wise beyond his years.

"Son, you ask too hard a question."[9]

Euriah Simpkins kept his daily trek near his young friend's home, and their deep conversations became Willie's education during those years.

"I learned early on to love him, to respect his every word as truth, and to watch his almost matchless conduct as a pattern," Willie said.[10]

"You're going to be a minister. God will provide." Circumstances might change, but their friendship and their talks never did. Their bond was strong.

Grandma Berry was right: God did make a miracle. It began when Mose Buffington heard of the Martha Berry School in Rome GA, where poor children could work for an education. Though he could not realistically spare his son's earnings from the sawmill, he sent him on.

"We'll find a way to make ends meet," Mose said.

With that, and $2.80 in his pocket, Willie rode the train some 300 odd miles to begin the 8th grade in November of 1925. He had not seen the inside of a classroom in nearly six years, but there was a drive, a

8

deep purpose that guided everything he did. For more than a year the boy studied and worked, digging sewers and picking up trash. That trash held treasures for Willie Lee. Old newspapers and magazines gave him more reading material than he ever saw in his life.

"I smoothed the pages out flat, clipped articles stories and pictures, then pasted them into notebooks. After I read them, they went straight home to Mr. Simpkins, useful tools for the poor Negro children he taught."

One of the school officials, looking out an office window, observed his unusual pastime, and recommended that he be moved to the library to work. In the monthly letters between the friends, Willie described the magical room where bookshelves were filled with biographies, histories, classical literature from the finest minds to ever live. Euriah answered every letter, and sent along a dollar from his meager $40 monthly salary. The boy, he knew, needed to purchase classroom supplies, and maybe shoes or pants, or a shirt and tie.

"I received my monthly letter from my Colored friend," Willie said, "chock full to the brim with good advice, just the kind a young man needs when he is away from the jurisdiction of home life, with encouragement that smoothed the hills of discouragement, and filled the valleys of despondency and made a highway upon which I was able to ride."[11]

Buffington did well enough academically that first year, except for the D Mrs. Hicks recorded next to his name in English Composition and Rhetoric during second term. Solid B's in both sessions of English History, Bible and Mathematics, and a C+ and B in Service were enough to offset his disappointment with two C+ in Agriculture. With A's in Work, Conduct, and Room (neatness), it added up to a good first year.

1926: Langston Hughes' *The Negro Artist and the Racial Mountain* is published. Hughes is a leader of the Harlem Renaissance.

"One can realize that Willie Lee Buffington was a hardworking and earnest student, as I can personally testify, he having been a student under my instruction," said Professor Earnest Buell of the Berry School.[12]

His second year at Berry began in the fall of 1927. Except for C+ in Algebra and Mechanical Drawing, he earned A's and B's in every other class. He even allowed himself the luxury of taking Band. G. Leland Greene, Principal of the school, spoke quite favorably of him.

"As a student he exhibited unusual energy and initiative. He was a leader in the campus life, particularly the religious interests, and always stood for the highest ideals."[13]

Overjoyed at young Willie's progress, Simpkins advised him to study hard and to take care of himself. Making up for lost time, the boy charged ahead, determined to make the Professor and his father proud. Under the strain of work, long hours of study, and longer hours of reading, Willie's health suffered. Exhausted, he was forced to withdraw from school, and on January 4th, 1928 he returned home.

He recuperated for six months in the care of his family, residing now in Ninety Six, South Carolina. Mose had journeyed from farmer to sawyer to textile worker. By the summer of that year, Willie was employed part-time in the mill, but also took an exam and was appointed a substitute mail carrier for the town. The young man found time to teach Sunday School at the Methodist church on the mill village.[14]

"Lintheads" were invariable wanderers, moving from mill to mill in search of a few more pennies on the hour, an easier job, or better living accommodations. It wasn't long before Mose had the family on the move again, this time to Calhoun Falls, most likely searching for all those things. "He was always looking for greener pastures, and he secured jobs there at the mill for him, me and my brother. Eight months we were there, and I think all the family got for its trouble was measles and pneumonia. What we left with was a big doctor bill.[15]

1929: 12 year old Dizzy Gillespie teaches himself to play the trumpet.

1929: *Hallelujah* is released, one of the first films to have an all-black cast.

"Somewhere, Daddy heard that the Kendall Company had bought the plant in Edgefield and was adding a night shift. The three men in the family went down there, met up with the mill superintendent, and we were hired. Daddy worked with steam engines while we were in the sawmill, and he was put to work as part of the shop crew. Luther went to the spooler room, and I headed for the weave room as a smash hand, an awkward sounding name for a pattern repairer."[16] His dexterity and aptitude soon led to a promotion as a loom fixer, the highest paying hourly job on the production floor. The family was home now, close to the land where they all grew up, close to the people they had known for most of their lives. And Willie was back with his old friend, who still believed the boy was destined for greater things than cotton mill work.

"I was the beneficiary of a golden friendship which continues to this day," he recalled later, "and as all good movements grow and prosper, this peculiar love Mr. Sim(p)kins had for me, and I for him, has become contagious, and has grown until I see no reason for the chasm that exists between the races in the South."[17] It was a belief he never relinquished.

He still remembered the dollar so sacrificially given, and the encouragement in Simpkins' letters during the dark days when his health suffered. Sometimes when he was alone, tears of sadness and frustration came because there was no way to repay the kindness shown. Along with the tears was a vow.

"Some day I'll find a way to pay it all back, find a way to pass it on. You'll see."[18] It was a promise he intended to keep.

Chapter 2 – "How can you have a school with no books?"

"It has always puzzled me how any Christian could claim the name of Christ and have ill will or hatred for any part of humanity. All my life I have battled with poverty and I am still of the opinion that the poor are not dishonorable. I know that it is possible to lead a noble, sweet, and rich life and be free from prejudice toward any race of God's creation. I wish every Negro girl and boy to have an opportunity to become a useful citizen."[19] Willie wasn't a politician, and never learned how to hide the truth when he spoke.

The events of the new decade were enough to destroy the dreams of even the strongest men. The Great Depression roared across the land, leaving in its wake breadlines and bankruptcies. Crushing debt was its legacy. Cole Blease geared his senate re-election campaign to a heightened racial hatred, determined to subjugate the entire African-American population through the fear of lynching. His primary support came still from the tenant farmers and citizens of the cotton mill villages. He never did one thing for them, but he sure could talk.

Into the teeth of that hatred walked young Mr. Buffington, taking up his accustomed post amid the deafening noise of the weave room. The white middle class viewed mill work as disgraceful, and assumed the workers lost their land due to laziness or stupidity. Working to help support his brother, sisters and parents, responsibilities grew even if his paycheck did not. He married his childhood sweetheart, Clara Rushton, on January 3rd, 1931, and the two set up housekeeping in a rented dwelling at 1206 Jones Street in Edgefield. Within a year, they had a son to care for.

March 25th, 1931: The nine Scottsboro (AL) Boys are arrested and charged with the rape of two white women. After trial, and re-trials, six are pardoned or have their convictions overturned. In 2013, the Alabama parole board grants posthumous pardons to the remaining three.

1931: Baseball great and Hall of Fame member Josh Gibson hits more than 70 home runs and leads the Homestead Grays of Pittsburgh PA to a 138-6 record.

There were big things happening in the Plum Branch community, courtesy of the Rosenwald School Program. Named after Sears & Roebuck president Julius Rosenwald, this matching grant fund provided for the construction of better quality schools for black children. Some

500 were built in South Carolina at a time when such support was woefully inadequate. Now, Professor Simpkins was going to have a new building in which to teach his students. The two friends walked the floor, smelled the fresh planed pine boards, admired the workmanship and the many educational improvements that awaited. But something was bothering Willie Lee.

"There are no books. How can you have a school with no books?"

"God will provide," his mentor reminded him. "He always does."

When Willie Lee had things on his mind, he walked. A lot troubled him as he made his way along the streets of Edgefield, and one more item was about to be added to his list. Something startled him from his reverie, and he looked up to see a middle-aged black woman coming toward him. She was holding the hand of a little boy, who suddenly bolted into the street, terrified at his approach.

"As if I were a wild animal; as if I should hurt him."[20]

Two things worked to lead Willie Lee Buffington toward a life of service to his African-American neighbors. First and foremost was his friendship with Euriah Simpkins, and second was the sight of a young black boy running into the street to avoid any contact with a white man. What was in motion now would alter the interracial landscape in the state. A lot of thinking still needed to be done, and hard times didn't make things any easier.

Growing up in the early part of the 20th century, it was expected of Buffington to embrace Jim Crow law, but he did not. He lived the life of a tenant farmer and a mill worker, and both experiences gave him an understanding of the hopelessness and complexities of poverty. His compassion for his black friends, and his Christian ethics, were instrumental in using his white privilege to effect reform for them.[21]

The Great Depression took its toll on people and businesses, and the "lintheads" at cotton mills often bore the brunt of reduced hours and low pay. Willie worked among the looms whenever the mill was open, keeping the belt-drive Draper E-models running and making first quality cloth. "A loom was my altar," he was fond of saying. Amid the noise and hot air, he wondered about Professor Simkpins' school and those empty bookshelves. Poor folks around Saluda had no books to speak of, and not much hope of ever getting them. Most rural communities in South Carolina were without any form of library service for either blacks or whites, but it was worse for his black friends. Conditions in the south were geared to prevent them from ever obtaining an adequate education and building a pathway out of their abject poverty. He wasn't prepared for the answer that came the way of a praying man, right there at that oddly situated altar.

"It was a startlingly vivid dream, one that the daylight could not make less real. I shut my eyes and saw the building in minute detail. I prayed and pondered over it, wondering if God still led men by dreams."[22]

Summer and autumn passed, and soon it was Christmas. Willie Lee worked when he could, and took his walks when the mill was on short time. The more he thought about Mr. Simpkins, the children, and the lack of books, the more dejected he became. He stuck his hands into his overall pockets.

And found a dime.

"Great, Willie. Just great. What can you do with a dime?" Twelve dollars a week doesn't go far providing for a family, and *anything* left over was a miracle. His walk took him to the steps of the Post Office. Not fully understanding why, he stepped inside, laid his coin on the counter, asked for five 2-cent stamps, and headed home.

Willie taught a Sunday School class at one of the local churches, and thumbing through the teacher's quarterly, he saw that the ministers who wrote the lessons provided their addresses. He chose five names and scratched out a letter. Part of it read, "The Negroes here have no books. Good books will help them more than anything else. I want to start a library for them. Could you send a book for it? Or, if you have none to spare, then please give me a stamp so that I can write to someone else." [23]

If he was home when the mail came, he asked the postman to check his bag one more time.

"Ain't nothing there, son. Done told you."

"Please? Just to be sure?"

The search always came up empty, and after a while Willie stopped asking. Two months passed, and in mid-February Clara stepped out to get the mail. Among the bills and flyers from the mill rested an odd envelope. Her bare feet slapped across the hardwood floor as she ran from the porch back to their little bedroom.

"Willie, you gotta see!"

Sitting on their bed and holding his son, he stared up at the letter in his wife's hand. It was from Harlem, in New York City. Reverend Lorenzo H. King, of St. Mark's Methodist Episcopal Church, provided the only answer to the letter writing campaign.

"I hope that you have not been interpreting our silence as a lack of interest in what you desire to do, for I can assure you that this is not true. I have presented your appeal for books to our congregation, and they keenly appreciate your interest in your Negro neighbors, and you will hear from us again. Already we have collected over 800 books, and

14

more are coming in each day. They will be shipped to you about April 15th."[24]

"When I get to the mill, I'll tell Dad, and he can take me over to see Mr. Simpkins tomorrow. Clara, the Professor's got to know first thing. These children will have books!"

1932: The Communist Party elects James W. Ford, an African-American, as its vice-presidential candidate.

1932: The New York Renaissance basketball team defeats the Boston Celtics for the locally billed World Championship.

Simpkins held the letter and smiled.

"God will provide, now and always, Willie Lee!" He took the hands of his friend between his rough ones. "The joy bells, they're starting to ring."

The books arrived, 1000 of them carefully packed in wooden barrels with the freight already paid. Willie and Euriah loaded their precious cargo onto the flatbed wagon pulled by mules and headed for Lockhart Baptist Church in Saluda. A meeting of the Negro community had been called, and folks were waiting. For so long, schools hereabouts didn't have even an old set of encyclopedias, and a whole classroom might use a single book for a history class, one child reading while others listened. And now, a treasure was bestowed upon Plum Branch.

"There are more here than the school will need." Mr. Simpkins ran his hand over one of the stacks of books carefully placed around the altar. "So what should we do? How do we make the best use of them?"

A reverent silence prevailed, and then one man, a father of six, spoke. "A library, that's what the community needs. That way, all the folks could use these books and learn to read." He looked up, first at Mr. Simpkins, then at Willie Lee. There were tears in his eyes, but a wondrous smile upon his face. Years of toil were wiped away just beholding the miracle of books and knowing what they might mean to his own children.

"We'll need a name," the Professor said.

"How about after you and Willie?" another man offered.

"No," both friends offered at the same time.

"This is bigger than two people, bigger than all of us!" Willie's voice captured the fervent emotion they all felt.

A young woman slowly stood, and licked her lips nervously. Emma Simpkins, Euriah's sister, was not accustomed to speaking before a large group. Her voice was quiet, but steady.

15

"We got logs. All of us together can build a cabin. Willie Lee and Mose, they know how to cut and plane boards. Folks about, black and white, will give a tree. All we had was faith to go on, faith in God and faith that what we are doing is right. Let it be Faith Cabin Library." It was seconded and passed by acclamation. And accompanied by more than a few "Hallelujahs".

A movement was born that day on the altar of a little church, in a community that probably didn't matter all that much to the world. Both blacks and whites did indeed donate timber. Purposely, more was cut than was needed, and the surplus sold to buy windows and doors. Friends gave their labor, and nothing was allowed to go to waste. The barrels in which the books were shipped were sawed in two and became chair bottoms. The women carefully upholstered cushions to fit snugly in the frames. An old piano, its sound board and strings long since mangled, was cut down, varnished, and became a perfect table. Rocks dug up in the fields were used by a stone mason, who happened to be Willie's father-in-law, to build an open fireplace and chimney. He charged for his unique labor, the only thing paid for with cash. He was called back for some additional work a few months later – to install concrete steps. The wooden ones were already worn out from constant use.

Beatrice Plumb and other authors quote an unnamed columnist comparing Julius Rosenwald and Buffington. "His (Rosenwald's) work is not so significant and outstanding as that of this Edgefield mill operator." Rosenwald was a millionaire, and Willie scraped by, barely providing for his family; Rosenwald operated from a distance, while Buffington was a neighbor to both black and white citizens who fought for survival during the Depression.[25]

It was a beautiful 18' x 22' structure dedicated the last day of 1932, raised up in faith, hope, and love. Books were sorted into sections designated for children, young people, and adults. A large area housed books on religious subjects, to be used by ministers of local churches.[26] Christened the Lizzie Koon Unit, after Buffington's mother, it caused quite a stir in the community and beyond. Above the fireplace, Willie put a sign fashioned from a piece of scrap lumber left over, and the one

The first Faith Cabin Library, shown abandoned in the 1970's.
The structure is no longer standing.
Courtesy Helen Norris and Ruby Barnes.

word etched there spoke volumes about him and Mr. Simpkins: OTHERS.

The festivities brought dignitaries who mingled with the local citizens. Dr. E.C. Peters, President of Paine College in Augusta GA, and his wife, Dr. Ethel Peters, attended, as did Dr. Ira C. Brown, Dr. Ruth Bartholomew, and W.C. Erwin. A letter was read from Reverend L.H. King, whose own passion for the library led to the first shipment of books from his Harlem church, and had never wavered.

"Your Faith Cabin project is one of the most beautiful and serviceable pieces of interracial cooperation in this country. It should have the support of the Metropolitan press in the widest possible publicity, with appeals for support."[27]

One official from the State Department of Education, reacting to the building and the pride shown by its builders, termed this first Faith Cabin Library "the rarest and most unique spiritual and intellectual institution in America." For Willie, it was much simpler. A dream, a dime, friends, and faith made it all possible. "Mostly faith," he would always say. He also crafted some words for the occasion:

"Faith Cabin Library, we dedicate you today, with all your rustic beauty and rich store of knowledge, to the glory of God and the uplift of mankind. May your influence spread far beyond these four walls and help youths and adults to grow and develop into men and women of great usefulness."

Buffington and Simpkins slipped away from the throngs of well-wishers, walking out into one of the nearby pastures. For a long time neither spoke, and after a while Simpkins reached out and squeezed the boy's shoulder.

"He always provides, son. God never stops keeping His promises."

"It mustn't end. It can't. There's still so much more to do, more folks who need this same kind of help, not just hereabouts, but in communities we've never heard of. There's just got to be..."

"A way," the Professor finished for his prized student, and his friend. "Your grandma had it right all those years ago, even before I knew you. God's still in the business of making miracles."

Barely a month later, Willie wrote to the NAACP with two requests. The first, obviously, was for more books..." so I wonder could you call for all the old text-books in a school in New York and send

18

them to a Country School about sixteen miles from this place...to be used by unfortunate pupils and kept as a school library."

The second asked for literature to fashion a lecture on "the advancement of 'Our Brothers of the Dark Continent'". Interestingly, Buffington noted that he used a Mirroscope Projector (presumably opaque) "in my lectures to social clubs, etc."[28] He had already moved beyond his letter-writing campaign and taken his dream to the citizens of Saluda and Edgefield. Practical prayer, after all, was more evident on the soles of one's shoes than on the worn knees of one's trousers.

There were other dreams being born along those rural backroads, and not just from the black children holding and reading the precious books. Every Friday, children from the white school at Plum Branch walked to the Faith Cabin Library to browse and check out books. Just maybe, such interaction was Willie's biggest dream of all.

Chapter 3 – "Let me not be my brother's keeper, but my brother's brother."

It is this proximity of Buffington to the racial problem and the fact that he himself is poor that makes the achievement of the man the more startling. His educational opportunities were indeed limited, he had no wealth except what he earned in the eternal whirl of cotton mill machinery and yet out of the often hidden fineness of human nature, out of the often ignored fact of the brotherhood of the human race he developed one of the most significant achievements in connection with the racial problem.

I.S. Caldwell[29]

"I heard Dr. John Lake, who was a Christian missionary to China, speak one evening," Buffington related on many occasions. As a young minister in Edgefield County, Lake was befriended by an older clergyman who lent him a book that changed the course of his life and led him halfway around the globe to serve for more than 30 years. "I resolved," said Buffington, "that if John Lake could go to China, I could serve at home."

Willie Lee Buffington[30]

As the first library rose from Saluda farmland that summer and autumn of 1932, word began to spread about what was going on. The local Klan most likely ignored it because the building would service only the Negro community around Plum Branch, and besides, it was named for a white woman whose elder son was a bit strange in his pursuits. But then, what could you expect from a "linthead" whose brain was pounded to mush every day by the thundering noise of looms?

Faith Cabin's reputation made its way to New York City, this time not to St. Mark's AME Church and Reverend King, but to the YMCA headquarters and Mr. Channing Tobias. A graduate of Paine College, he was a most remarkable man. After a six-year tenure as professor of Bible Literature at his alma mater (1905-1911), Tobias began a long association with the Young Men's Christian Association, holding a number of positions with the organization from 1911 through 1946. He left to become the first black director of the Phelps-Stokes Fund, devoted to improving educational opportunities for African-

Americans. President Harry Truman appointed him to the Committee on Civil Rights in 1946, and in 1953 Tobias continued service to his country as an alternate representative to the United Nations. That same year, he was elected chairman of the National Association for the Advancement of Colored People.

Starting in 1932, and continuing for ten years, Tobias and Buffington corresponded with one another regularly, and the letters were a window into the development of the young man at the hands of another wise mentor. Though no one could ever take the place of Euriah Simpkins in Willie Lee's life, Tobias became for him an advisor whose professional standing went far beyond anything he could imagine. The letters revealed a young man passionately searching for ways to fulfill the mission of making books available to a whole society who had no access, and even less hope of ever obtaining them.

"For the past five years, in my spare time, like the weekends etc., I have been doing mission work among the colored folks in rural districts," he wrote.[31]

Buffington, unlike so many who were willing to pursue causes when support was solid and the inflow of income posed no problems, did not wait for the attention of foundations and made no demands for legislation or public funds. He looked upon a scene of intellectual devastation and described clearly what his African-American friends, and, by definition, himself, must overcome.

"At the present prices of farm commodities they are almost unable to pay their taxes, and many of them do not have the necessities of life. With more than 200 eager, ambitious boys and girls in school, and more of school age in the community who cannot attend because of no clothing and books, with more than 100 of school age, but have been forced to stay and help with the ever increasing burden at home, I reviewed the possibilities of a small library for the school and community, as I saw that the overcrowded rooms were bare as far as books were concerned."[32]

He described the construction of that first library to Tobias, the methods of contacting donors and arranging for shipment (the results of his letter writing campaign in December of 1931) and boldly asserted his belief in the ultimate success of Faith Cabin Libraries. There was no Dungeon of Doubting Castle here.

"I seriously trust that you will not let the simplicity of the plan and the feebleness of the letter induce you not to take steps about this matter...Some day when this work gets in the hands of the proper party and develops into a School strong for God and His Holy Word you will be glad that you had a part in it."[33]

"People with such power, Uncle Eury, do they listen to poor men like us?" They paused from their work, stacking more rocks so the stone mason could resume work on the fireplace and chimney first thing in the morning. "There's so much that needs doing beyond Plum Branch. Can people so far away care at all?"

Simpkins took a drink of coffee and passed the cup to Willie. As was their custom, they shared everything from hopes and dreams to coffee and biscuits. "This man knows about the South. He taught at Paine College, remember. And like Reverend King, they got heartstrings that feel the tug. Wonderful things are happening, Willie. Look at the faces around you, the hopes and expectations that make all this work joyful. And like I say…"

"Yes", and they laughed together as Willie finished his sentence, "God will provide." The last of the coffee gone now, they finished unloading the wagon as the moon came up over the fields. The unfinished library cast a long shadow in the cool evening light.

Some three weeks passed, and Willie had nervous energy to burn waiting for an answer to his letter. Euriah tried to tell him that Mr. Tobias was a busy man, and that the YMCA was a big organization, but nothing slowed his young friend's pacing.

"At this rate, we'll build five more libraries before that letter's even got a chance to get here."

"Ten," the boy threw back over his shoulder, carrying some more boards to the men waiting to nail them in place. The next afternoon, everybody for miles around knew that Willie Lee got his answer. No one could miss the figure bolting across the plowed rows toward the Simpkins' homestead, the letter clutched tightly in his hand.

"Your good letter of October 11th touched me very deeply; in fact to such an extent that I have referred to it in connection with devotional services and public addresses that I have delivered since I received it. I wish you all possible success in your laudable efforts to serve the spiritual and intellectual interests of others of your community less fortunate that yourself." [34]

"Most boys from down south go a lifetime and never get a letter from important folks in New York City, and here you got two in a year!" Euriah was no good trying to hide how proud he was of his young friend. "You'll be right back in touch with him, I'm expecting."

"Soon as we finish getting the library in the dry, guess that's about right."

"Don't work yourself to death, son. Man's got to rest, spend some time with his wife and baby boy. Can't just be going from this job to fixing on that set of looms you run in the mill. We're in this 'til the finish. Let's go get some supper and find you a ride back to Edgefield." He didn't take 'no' for an answer, not this time.

Next evening, Willie was at the kitchen table, pounding on his old typewriter. He wasn't fast, and it took a few hours to complete his response under a bare electric bulb that popped, fizzed, and blinked now and then when the November wind kicked up. The tone of his writing, borne of gratitude flavored with hero worship, certainly waxed poetic.

"Your splendid letter of the 5th, which was royally welcomed upon my part, should have had my special attention before now, yet my work in the mill is so hard until I can't sit up late every night...Words are not at my command to adequately express to you my heartfelt thanks and appreciation to you for the interest you have made manifest in your splendid, yea, valuable letter."[35] Sometimes he revealed an item or two about his private life, such as when he was able to have finally saved a few dollars, only to have them diverted to paying for his baby boy's emergency tonsillectomy.

And Willie was something of a prophet in his postscript, considering what his library building program would one day accomplish.

"Oh! If I had all the old idle books in New York City tonight, we would have to build a dozen Faith Cabins to hold them. I am so grateful to you for your interest."[36]

Tobias was impressed enough with young Buffington that the two agreed to meet at Paine College in early February, 1933. Surely it was a passionate outpouring from the pupil to the teacher, and yet there was already much evidence that the boy meant what he said. Even a busy man like Tobias must pay attention. A February 13th letter from Buffington provided a view of the day's activities.

"I cannot express enough to you the feeling I had when you spoke (the) first time to me in St. John's Church, when you said, 'I recognize your face.' That day, and those words are written upon the tablets of my heart."[37] Buffington spoke of his Faith Cabin effort at Plum Branch, of the inquiries to build a second one at Ridge Spring, and of his dream of seeing these libraries throughout the South.

"Another reflection upon the soul of my native South is that Negroes are denied the use of their public libraries."[38] The men talked of the realities of their lives, though young Willie was the more vocal.

"When I am away from home, as in the case of Wednesday, I am losing what it takes for me to keep up and going, yet I feel that I was well repaid for the day's work. Even with a scanty dinner which the wife prepared before I left, for I didn't fell (sp) able to buy lunch, I was happy and satisfied."[39]

23

Willie closed with a glimpse of his family life.

"When I left home Wednesday morning, my wife said: 'If Dr. Tobias can see Faith Cabin this P.M., you bring him by home for supper before returning to Augusta.' She was certainly disappointed when I came back and said it was impossible for you to get away.'"[40] Tobias proved a staunch ally of the young man, and like Simpkins offered a broader introduction to the battle for civil rights.

Tobias rubbed shoulders with giants in the growing movement, and this early correspondence shed light on the kind of reaction Willie's work brought from his co-workers at Edgefield's Kendall Mill. The firebrand racial politics of Cole Blease still held sway among the "lintheads". They may have indulged what they saw as Buffington's misbegotten passion in providing a library out at a dirt road crossing where no one was the wiser. But when another took shape in Ridge Spring not long after, and a third in Newberry (the stronghold of Blease himself) just a short time later, the work became a danger to be reckoned with. Upsetting the social order was not acceptable.

Those early years in the 1930's, Willie Lee was at the mill ready to work when the whistle blew to signal shift change. When the mill ran full time, he put in 54 hours a week, bringing home $12 that somehow stretched to support his wife and baby boy, and pay the rent. In the letters of 1932, he wrote to Tobias of laboring among the looms and then working into the night on the Faith Cabin project.

"Remember me as a poor Cotton Mill boy, working every day, then sitting up at night working for others of your race. Poor, yet glad and happy to do what I can for them and my Master."[41]

A month later, upon being told by Tobias that the letters were shared with others, he wrote,"...(you) who will take a letter written at night by a poor insignificant cotton mill boy, and read parts of it to great and influential men in the great city of New York..."[42]

By February, 1933, the concerns became monetary as well.

"I am not sure as yet that I can attend (Tobias was to speak at Paine College during the Easter season), as my wages are so meager until I can hardly keep even and work full time."[43] He continued in the same letter,

"I assure you that I am doing all that I possibly can, and still work in the mill, without compensation. I have not been able to retire a single night within the past year until after 10 o'clock, after a hard day's work among the looms."[44]

Buffington did attend the Paine College convocation that February, and made the acquaintance of Dr. Will Alexander. Some fourteen years earlier, after one of the worst race riots in recent memory erupted in Arkansas, Alexander established the Commission on Interracial Cooperation in Atlanta. Unity, he reasoned, must start somewhere, and 1919 in Georgia was as good a place as any.

Returning home from Augusta, Willie began correspondence with Dr. Alexander, and though it would reach neither the magnitude nor the influence of that with Channing Tobias, the young man's passion for the cause of civil rights and equality were palpable.

"I enjoyed the things you told the Missionary Council in St. John's Church at the Morning session," he wrote February 15th, answering the doctor's letter. "I shall tell you more in my story about my stand for Right and Justice to all races.

"I am a mill worker," he continued, "laboring under the famous 'stretch-out' system so familiar to the legislative assemblies at this time."[45] 'Lintheads' had their hands full battling owners who demanded that weavers and spinners run more looms and frames on their jobs, a major factor in the efforts to unionize the industry during the mid-1930's.

Another letter soon made its way toward Atlanta four days later; whether as a response to Alexander's reply (the timing suggests not), cannot be determined. Willie's dedication to the work he has chosen was unmistakable.

"I could relate many interesting stories to you about my contact with Negroes, and about arguments with my white friends...," he wrote, wanting Dr. Alexander to know "that I believe the Negro is not getting a square deal, and that I am willing to give my life in service to remedy the existing evils." And it was not only *his* efforts that he pledged. "Nevertheless, my wife is willing to sacrifice and suffer with me in the cause which I foster," and "that in the near future we shall see plans develop whereby the South will be blessed with hundreds of such Faith Cabins."[46]

A letter on March 3rd, 1933 underscored his desire to discuss "how I might be able to go further with this work, and possibly with my education, that I might be able to render more and better service to my country."[47]

His final letter was dated April 10th, imploring Dr. Alexander, much as he had done with Channing Tobias, to use his position and status to help spread the word. "I must, under present conditions, depend upon [influencial] men, who travel to tell some others about Faith Cabin, since I am poor, must work every day and then can hardly make ends meet, cannot travel in the interest of this work, and by staying at home one rarely meets anyone interested in Negro education and racial understanding sufficiently to help."[48] When it came to the Faith Cabin

Library movement, Willie sought and seized every opportunity to expand the work, and he was not shy about letting others, "influencial" or not, know what they could do to help.

Circumstances turned more ominous with the coming of spring. He was still content with his work, but co-workers viewed him much differently.

"The world needs men," Euriah Simpkins said, and it would take a man to stand against the prejudice and hatred simmering beneath the surface in Edgefield.

"Nothing serious has loomed up as yet, however vision tells me there is a vast difference in the folks for whom I work and upon whom I depend in an indirect way, for my livelihood. I can see it, I can feel it," he confided to Tobias. "Since the day this work (Faith Cabin Libraries) became known in the two counties, by local newspapers, I have noticed the attitude of my white *fair-weather acquaintances* for certainly they could not be called Friends, when so little a matter could cause such a break. I never feared them, and still do not."[49]

Later in the same letter, Buffington detailed the alienation he felt. His father, brother, and half-sister worked in the mill during this time. Did they sense the same dangers? Were they warned to stay away?

"I certainly get the hand of the boss upon my shoulder with words of praise concerning the manner that I run my work, etc., however, I find my favors and privileges about the plant being cut off, and a constant tightening up of things for me, which I am proned (sp) to think is intended to make me quit after extended time. I have decided I will not be provoked, but rather take it all easy, work some harder to satisfy the ones I work for. As for promotion, I shall never get that here. Just this past week I saw a handsome demonstration of that."[50] We can only wonder what that demonstration was.

Persevering in spite of injustice became his strategy to change Jim Crow society once and for all.

"Sometimes the days get dark, don't they, boy?" He hadn't noticed as Euriah made his way toward the steps of the library. It was easy to come here and get lost in the dreams stirred up by Faith Cabin, and it rested his mind after long and lonely days in the mill.

"Doesn't get any better, that's for sure." Willie Lee smiled back at his closest friend who always came around at the right time. "Lots of folks figure they can make my life miserable, and if they do a good enough job, then I'll leave all this behind, come to my senses," he looked back at the library, "and stop trying to fix what I see as humanity at its worst."

The hand on his shoulder was filled with strength, and he still winced when Euriah gave a squeeze. But it was always welcomed.

"Evil, son, has never known color, nor gender, nor much else except ways to infect people's thinking. And usually it's best when starting up some kind of warfare between folks who have every reason to work together and love each other, but just don't. Look at us here. Black, white, neither has much money and mostly we just barely scrape by. Not many well-equipped schools, very few libraries, and even with all this, we maintain two separate educational systems, and we're all the poorer for it."

Willie just waited. The usually quiet Uncle Eury didn't sermonize often, but when he did, his pronouncements were eloquent. The boy knew there would be time for questions. Now was a time for listening.

"This thing you got yourself into, young man, is a great and worthy undertaking. But don't ever get fooled thinking this world is going to appreciate it much, if at all. What I've found in my life is, when you start getting close to making things better for folks who have been having a hard time, making a dream of yours come true that helps people, that's when evil flexes its muscles and opposition rises up all around you." Euriah sat down next to Willie. Early spring winds kicked up as darkness fell, and had a chill about it.

"I wrote Mr. Tobias not long ago and told him all of this was just air castles right now, coming from a poor boy working and praying among the noisy looms in a South Carolina cotton mill."[51]

"Not for some people. Your dream is very real to them, Willie Lee. My little sister named this Faith Cabin Library, and she couldn't read on that night we stacked those books on the church altar. But she can now, and so can a whole lot of other folks who maybe once was scared to learn, 'cause it was kept from them for so long. They ain't scared now, son, 'cause of what you do and how you care. It shows, and this," he stood up and look over his shoulder at the library, "it may not be a castle, but its foundation is strong enough to support one."

27

Chapter 4 – "Reach the unreached and help the unhelped."

"I was told on the day of Dedication of Faith Cabin by some old Negroes who knew my (paternal) grandfather that he loved Negroes better than any white man they ever knew. He, being poor, never owned any land in his life, yet he helped build the little Community Church for Negroes by denying his family the use of some Cotton seed (which were 8 cents per bushel) and donating them to the building fund."[52]

Willie Buffington

Willie reached out, further than he ever had, to leaders of the black community who understood just where this idea of building libraries could lead. Much as he did in contacting Channing Tobias, he cultivated another friendship, this time a bit closer than New York City.

"I have recently found a great friend in the person of Professor A.W. Nicholson, Bettis Academy, Trenton South Carolina, and go often now to confer with him. He tells me you (Tobias) have written him about Faith Cabin Library. He is at present having made, at the School, some letter heads for me, which will be of added emphasis to my letters and appeals...I learned to love him this first visit, and now regard him as one of the greatest men I know."[53]

The measure of a man's greatness lay with what was in his heart and nothing else, according to Willie Lee. Those "letter heads" served to continue young Buffington's "faith and a dime" writing campaign, reaching people who donated books and made possible the founding of more Faith Cabin libraries. Nicholson, born into slavery just before the end of the Civil War, became a very specific role model. Like him, Buffington would lose himself in teaching black students, giving himself to them later in his life. Saying good-bye to his friend after one visit, the old man who spent 53 years serving the young people of Bettis Academy offered words that burned in Willie's mind and never went away:

"We are trying to reach the unreached and help the unhelped."[54]

Willie understood the impassioned directive, and often asked himself: "Is the world better because I have lived in it? All my days... I have tried to answer that in the affirmative."[55]

Nicholson's kindness did not go unrewarded. Four years after their friendship began, Bettis was given the largest endowment of books up to that time, thanks to a Buffington letter that reached ministers in Iowa City IA. The local *Press-Citizen* ran a story in 1937 of the Faith Cabin Library Club, Mrs. L.H. Pierce presiding.

"Bettis Academy has been chosen as the site of the Iowa City Unit...Of the 300 students who live in the community, some walk six or seven miles to school. There was a bus to transport these, but the Depression forced its cancellation."

Buffington praised these students and the school.

"The quality of the instruction and the spirit of the teachers make the graduates outstanding. Bettis Academy grads are in demand with the department of education in South Carolina!"[56]

Buffington was confident enough to specify both the need and the outcome of Faith Cabin Libraries in his letters. "They pursue a well-rounded source of information, and ask for fiction (both classics and modern), history, biography, Bible study, travel, reference work, gift subscriptions to good magazines, and especially children's books." He goes on to add, "You will be making an investment in Christian character...an investment that will yield dividends throughout all eternity."[57]

There was a growing interest in this peculiar practice of building libraries along the backroads of the south. People wanted to know more about Willie, and many wanted a part in what he was doing. Bessie Drew, the managing editor of *Southern Workman* at the Hampton Institute in Virginia, asked him to tell of this pioneering work for her magazine.[58] A church in Kinston NY notified him that they were sending a large shipment of books for another Faith Cabin Library, whenever he started building it.[59] And Willie took some time to motor to Augusta and visit with Paine College president Dr. E.C. Peters, moments that he truly enjoyed. As in his exchanges with A.W. Nicholson, Willie learned more about himself.

"I have within my heart an inward burning to bury, or lose my life in just such work as I find at Paine College."[60]

"But how?" He wondered aloud as he returned home that Saturday evening. "A poor man who works in a cotton mill, barely making enough money to care for his wife and son, hasn't finished high school, and wants to teach in college. That about sums it up, right?' The wind through the open car window tousled his hair, and its coolness kept him awake as he maneuvered along the dark road on a moonless night.

Library at Bettis Academy. The building remains standing.
Courtesy Dan Lee.

He often regained his bearings in the exchange of letters with his mentors, in this case Channing Tobias. One on March 21, 1933, showed the kinds of people who helped him make sense of his life's work.

"I will not fail to call Dr. Sherwood Eddy's name as you suggested. You can relate to him the story. Tell him I was a student when he was at The Berry School, Rome Georgia, and that I remember very vivid his lectures and count their teachings very valuable to me, since they saved me many pitfalls in life I am sure."[61] Eddy was a Protestant missionary who, in 1911, was appointed National Secretary of the YMCA for Asia. He and Tobias would have been well acquainted.

Willie was busy. Building libraries and providing for his family were honorable, worthwhile things, and either constituted a full-time job for almost any other man. But he was troubled. To truly answer what he had been called to do, he needed a college education. He wrote again to Dr. Tobias.

"Just a few nights ago I dreamed I was going away to College on foot, without money and by faith. If I ever get to go it will be by faith, unless the miraculous happens."[62]

His long letter to Tobias on March 25th returned again and again to that very matter. He spoke of the efforts to build libraries, saying that "I would be happy to give my full time to the establishing of such institutions all over the South". Yet, he feared that his correspondence asking for donations of books was not of sufficient power to bring results. He talked passionately about helping at a level far more than bricks and mortar.

"My interest in the Negro and the injustices under which he lives cannot be fake…If I might assure you that I am truly able only to offer sincerity, for that is all I possess…"

Yet,

"I am not anxious for anyone to give me anything. I have been working since I was five years old, and don't mind it a bit."[63]

The work may not have scared him, and with what Buffington had experienced in his lifetime it probably didn't. But the idea of school at his age, and what he lacked in formal education, carried a measure of intimidation.

"I know how to be practical but with 1½ years of High School work, I fear the future in a field as complicated as race relations."[64]

He begged his friend for guidance as to what path he should take. Rather than try to answer such questions in a letter, Tobias' wise response was that they needed to meet face-to-face. With fortunate timing, that meeting was not far off.

During Easter week, Tobias was back in Augusta, lecturing and fundraising for his alma mater. The two talked about the young man's future, and though Willie desired that education, he remained more comfortable in the library work, though he lamented, "I am daily burdened with the thought of the little I am able to do."[65] That burden drove him, not only to keep up his backbreaking schedule week after week, but to set right the injustices he encountered daily.

"Until I am offered a way to climb higher, be sure that I will be found upon the job all along...developing the present and any other Cabins we might be able to establish, meeting (sp) out to those I see treated so unjustly, just what I would appreciate if I were in their position."[66]

Their families also got acquainted during this visit. Willie expressed his delight in meeting Mrs. Tobias, and had the opportunity of introducing them to his parents, though he apologized for the elder Buffington being the reason they could not spend more time together.

"...my father has a horror of driving at night, and more so since South Carolina has unrestricted beer."[67]

Tobias also gave a talk on the radio sometime that week, and Willie walked to his father's house so the two of them could listen together. The crystal set was a luxury the younger man could not afford.[68]

Willie's co-workers at the mill, and many of his neighbors, did not support him at all in his endeavors, and his fellow "lintheads" were openly hostile to him. But he did get support from his parents, especially his father. Mose did much more that accompany his son on that Easter trip to Paine College in 1933. He also helped Willie in the collection of his books, offered his street address as the drop point for the donations, and, in his own way reached out to the people Willie loved so deeply.

He sponsored an essay contest that spring among the African-American boys and girls of the community, with the subject "What Faith Cabin Library Means To Me". The two prize winners (one boy, one girl) received a free day trip to Augusta GA, and the Columbia *State* published the essays. The young man wrote in part:

"...the library means so much to me because it was established by one of our southern white friends in the person of Mr. Willie Lee Buffington. Born and reared not far from the present site of the Faith Cabin, I appreciate his efforts in trying to bring my Negro race to the light through books. I will never forget him and will always love him. After all, whatever I received from the Faith Cabin Library, I can use it and carry it with me until death."[69]

In much the same way, the young woman shared her thoughts:

"I cannot conclude unless I mention something about Mr. Buffington. Common sense teaches me that Mr. Buffington is a great man because he is doing great things for me. He is earnest, thoughtful and has good religion; and good remembrances, and above all keeps in touch with God, so that he will help me to do great things. I pray for Mr. Buffington to go forward like he is doing."[70]

"God still makes the miracle, Willie Lee," he would hear as he made his way among the looms. But who knew that the Almighty would enlist the federal government to do His bidding?

The National Relief Act (NRA) came along in 1933, as the government cut working hours in the mill from eleven in a day to eight. Edgefield, like so many cotton mills, went to a three shift operation: 6:00AM – 2:00PM, 1st shift; 2:00PM – 10:00PM, 2nd shift; and 10:00PM – 6:00AM, 3rd shift.

"Something's happening here, and it's opening doors," he told Mr. Simpkins, the two sitting at the supper table. Clara smiled as she scooted past, young Willie Jr. in her arms, bathed and ready for bed.

"Don't you let him stop, Professor. Push him, push him hard."

"Somehow, by that look on his face, won't be no need. He's done been pushed, and things in motion now can't nothing on this earth stop. Rest easy on that, Clara."

Willie was assigned second shift, and in August took the opportunity to visit Edgefield High School and talk to superintendent T.H. Nelson. Could a married man, he asked, return to school? With the approval of the school board secured, Nelson gave his blessings, and at age 24, Buffington started to school again. A husband, father, loom fixer, Faith Cabin Library director and school boy, he stepped onto the road he was meant to travel, with a work schedule that would have led most men to an early grave. He relished it all, kicking his letter-writing campaign to donors into high gear.

"This letter was due to be issued last weekend – as I must use weekends to attend to Faith Cabin Library's affairs – since I am in School, and in the mill each day of the week."[71]

He was at school in the morning and early afternoon, then went home to change clothes, picked up lunch and a mason jar of sweet tea that Clara packed, and headed to the mill until his shift ended late that night. In those weekends of letter writing, he shared his life.

"Yes, I am liking school fine to be so advanced in age. It takes courage to attend Class each day with mere children – not to speak of trying experiences I must pass through. A good friend in New York City sent me a check to help me enter all the School activities this year."[72] Three of the book donors that year – Albert Stamm, Oberlin College (Ohio) and Haverford College (Pennsylvania) – would eventually have Faith Cabin Library units named after them. All that studying late at night, after a full day of school and work, paid off handsomely. The Edgefield *Advertiser* carried the Honor Roll for the 10th grade in early November – Miss Helen Mims, Miss Daisy Gibson, and Mr. Willie L. Buffington.

As a high school student, he was invited to one of the Christian Student Conferences held at Paine College, though he could not recall whether it was in 1934 or 1935. "What I learned and saw was a contributing factor in my decision to attempt to do more to right the wrong that existed…do something NOW about improving relationships between whites and blacks."[73]

Folks in other states took notice of this ambitious young man, who stood out among his classmates at school and who was left pretty much to himself in the mill. The first major article to appear was George Kuyper's "An Adventure In Faith". Kuyper was a faculty member at the Hampton Institute in Virginia.

"The more opportunity to peruse the printed page in quiet and comfortable surroundings will prove a benediction to many who come from poor cabins. Spread Faith Cabins not only throughout the rural sections of the South but also in congested urban quarters and a miracle of race adjustment will ultimately take place."[74]

A phrase that made its way into many publications, among them the Columbia *State* newspaper, noted that "inter-racial relations would improve far faster in South Carolina if there were more Willie Lee Buffingtons." The *State* thought enough of Buffington's work to have 1000 copies of the article printed and donated for his public relations releases. The Richmond *Times-Dispatch*, though, chose a more raw approach to convey its editorial point of view.

"It is unfortunately true that many of the white tenant farmers in the Southern States are inclined to be hostile to the Negroes, in direct contrast to the attitude of Mr. Buffington."[75]

I.S. Caldwell, whose son Erskine proved to be a caustic social critic of southern racism and other deviations in such writings as *God's Little Acre* and "Saturday Afternoon", challenged a whole generation of white readers in a column for the Augusta *Herald*, entitled "Bread Cast Upon The Waters Is Returning".

"Bright young people are prone to think that there is nothing great left undone, that there is no chance for pioneer enterprise. It is thought by these young people that one cannot expect to achieve a unique career without money and the opportunities that money will buy. The experience of Willie Lee Buffington is proving that doors of opportunity are ready to be opened at the least expected places."[76]

There was growing recognition that this young man possessed ideas capable of changing the way people thought about race relations. Buffington pursued his dream because it was the right thing to do. "We are all God's children", he was fond of saying, a simple truth he felt should be readily apparent to everyone. Simple truth was seldom accepted readily, if at all, and the "miracle of race adjustment" proved to be a long and bitter struggle.

There was no time to squeeze anything else into his busy life when he received a short note from Mr. Simpkins, asking him to come to the Lockhart Church Wednesday evening coming. It was Revival Week, and in addition to preaching and singing, some people from Ridge Spring were traveling over to talk with them.

"Another castle, I believe," was the closing sentence.

Groundbreaking for what became the Annie Bodie Unit occurred that autumn at the Rosenwald School near Ridge Spring. The old school had not been allowed to issue high school diplomas at that time due to regulations requiring a library to be available to students. But when the Faith Cabin Library opened January 1st, 1934, the school was fully accredited and the awarding of sheepskins approved. The WPA (Works Progress Administration, part of President Roosevelt's New Deal) supplied the labor to erect the building, and the school principal and board of trustees collected donations and raised other money for the furnishings. Buffington and Simpkins delivered more than 2000 books. Dr. E.C. Peters, Paine College president, delivered the dedicatory address, saying he knew of "no more unique inter-racial enterprise."[77]

A Ridge Spring resident, Reverend John Watson, wrote to Buffington, who reproduced the letter to send to Faith Cabin Library supporters. Watson talked of people working together toward a wondrous goal.

"Now that a project has been started in Ridge Spring, all the public spirited citizens know that the sane thing to do is to push with all

Buffington delivering books from the back of the Jeep station wagon.
Courtesy Caroliniana Library.

their might to complete it. The cooperation offered by our white friends here is wonderful. Faith Cabin Libraries will give our rural boys and girls a chance to know something of the outside world, things they will hardly have a chance to know through travel and experience."[78] Watson also found personal benefits from using the library.

"I preached a sermon based upon the material in one of the books – and the folks who heard me preach commented that it was the best sermon they had ever heard me expound."[79]

In her writings on the Faith Cabin Library movement, Beatrice Plumb looked to the future, and how different it might be because a generation was given the gift of books.

"When they leave...who knows what good seed has been sown in those youthful minds. They go back to their poor little dwellings, dreaming dreams..."[80]

1934: The Dust Bowl devastates the plains of the American Midwest.
Ella Fitzgerald debuts at the Apollo Theater in Harlem NY.

As months passed, the libraries offered more and more to their communities. Book clubs began, and children reviewed current events, gave book reports, and raised money to buy books by black authors. Graduates moved on to college, better prepared because books were a part of their lives. One of the local Baptist churches used the facility for religious conferences, and soon electricity was added by the REA, making possible the use of a radio-phonograph.[81]

Mr. Simpkins smiled as he reflected on another biblical truth made real – the people who had walked in darkness had seen a great light. And it was guiding them along pathways no one could have imagined.

The third Faith Cabin Library followed closely, completed in 1935. Located at Newberry's new Drayton Street School, it was named the L.H. King Unit, honoring the pastor of St. Mark's Methodist Church in Harlem, the only man who answered Willie's first letter of appeal. The books were surplus volumes from the recently established Annie Bodie Unit, as the movement spread for the first time outside Saluda County. People started hearing the testimonials offered by those whose lives were transformed.

"I am entering my fourth year as a student at Drayton Street High School...I have read with great pleasure and profit the following books from the Faith Cabin Library in our school (Langston Hughes' *Not*

Without Laughter; Marc Connelly's *Green Pastures*; Swift's *Gulliver's Travels*; Twain's *Adventures of Huckleberry Finn*).

"Throughout my three years' study our library has been a great help to me in solving my problems in school, and in helping me to form the habit of using my leisure time in a profitable way." -Signed Rosalie Gilliam[82]

The library staff also loaned books and magazines to four other rural schools in Newberry County.

His dark fingers stroked the soft pale cheek of Ethel Buffington, born April 2, 1935. She slept in Clara's arms as the two men stood by the bed. After a while, they sat on the porch steps, the breeze carrying the sounds of shuttles clacking in the looms at the mill.

"A month away from high school graduation, young man, and now the father of two beautiful children. This life of yours is getting near full of miracles and the responsibilities that go with them. You've been given a lot, boy, and there's a lot you can give back."

Willie looked up at the stars, listened as the noise from the mill filled the night air, and sighed at the wonder of it all.

Chapter 5 – Pressed for time: husband, father, college student, library founder, grocery clerk, ordained minister.

"Willie Lee Buffington." Mr. Nelson's voice carried through the warm auditorium, calling from his seat a loom fixer, a husband, a father, a builder of libraries, and now a high school graduate. There was polite applause. At the back stood the best friend this young man would ever know, his big hands lifted toward heaven, his head bowed. He cried softly, tears of joy splashing on the scuffed hardwood floor. Mr. Simpkins brushed the tears away as the next name was called, respectfully stood until the ceremony ended, and slipped out into the night.

Dr. E.C. Peters, Paine College president, watched the graduation that evening, and later told Buffington that he would try to hire him as a teacher when his college education was completed.[83] Ernest Buell, who had taught Willie during his time at the Martha Berry School, stopped on his trip home to Connecticut to watch his former student reach this first educational milestone. And a letter came from Dr. B.E. Geer, president of Furman College in Greenville SC, inviting him to enroll there for the fall semester. But arrangements were already made, and the Buffingtons were on their way to Spartanburg and a new home at Wofford College.

For all the careful planning, though, Willie's post-high school education was not destined for the Hub City. Wofford College president Dr. Snyder assisted the Buffingtons with finding a house and Willie with finding employment at Spartan Mill, a local textile company. But this job was more than the young man could handle.

"I worked for two weeks at Spartan Mill. The first week I worked I realized if I worked at the job they gave me I had no energy left to study. You could track me from the mill where I worked down the sidewalk to where I lived from the sweat that was running off my overalls when I was going home every morning. I was working at night and just had no energy left."[84]

The experience led to another serious conversation with Dr. Snyder. Yes, he understood about the problems at work, but this was 1935, and jobs were not there to be picked over. Yes, he would do what he could to help, but for the life of him he did not know what that could be.

"Before you take this step, young man, think it through. There might not be another opportunity out there."

Faced with hard decisions that held no readily apparent solutions, Willie Lee did what always worked for him in such circumstances. He prayed. And he wrote letters. The first was to his old friend, not so much for advice (he knew what that would be), but to clear his head. Talking with Euriah brought things out of the shadows and made them easier to understand.

"They moved me to the slasher room, and mixing the yarn sizing liquid in a cooking kettle, keeping the yarn untangled over and under the drying drums, tying back the broken ends – all that in an area way hotter than the weave room. It just takes it all out of me."

Moths banged against the back screen door. He had a small desk set up outside the bedroom so he would not disturb Clara and the babies, and used two candles for his light. Willie hunkered down over his paper. The pencil scratching across it soothed his thoughts.

"The best advice you ever gave me was that what happened to a man fits together, and if you looked careful enough you could begin to make out the big picture. Folks here are nice. Dr. Snyder has listened to me like a daddy, and Clara makes the best of it for us. But in my heart I know I'm not supposed to be here. I'll stay here and work as long as it takes, but I'm going to write Dr. Geer at Furman and see maybe if I can speak with him about attending there. But God will provide. Yes, I see your smile. Even far away, you're a good listener. Thank you. Your friend, Willie Lee."

He blew the candles out, stuffed the pages into an envelope and slid it into his overall pocket. He'd mail it on his way home. Closing the back door, he set out for the mill just as one of the clocks in town chimed 9 o'clock.

In the morning, after another long, hot shift, he ate breakfast with Clara and held Willie Jr. and Ethel as they stirred awake. Before taking a bath and going to bed, he wrote to Dr. Geer, asking if Furman might still accept him as a student.

That letter prompted action from the moment it arrived. Geer did not wait to answer by mail, but sent his secretary on a mission to find an available telephone connection close to the Buffington residence in Spartanburg.

"It belonged to a woman we did not know who lived six houses up the street," Willie said. "The call came one morning about 8:30AM, and she walked down to tell me there was a call from Furman."

The two men arranged to meet that afternoon at 2:00PM in the President's office on campus. Buffington took the Piedmont and Northern electric railroad from Spartanburg to Greenville. He made the meeting, accepted Dr. Geer's offer, including the front two rooms of a house near campus (they would have the entire dwelling when the current resident, a senior, graduated), and in August of 1935 began his college career.[85] It was a move neither the men nor the institution ever regretted.

May, 1935: Cartoonist Oliver Harrington begins his "Dark Laughter" strip in New York City's *Amsterdam News*.

June, 1935: In the court case Murray vs. Pearson, NAACP attorneys Thurgood Marshall and Charles Hamilton Houston successfully argue to open admissions to the University of Maryland School of Law on the basis of equal protection under the 14th Amendment of the Constitution.

The family settled in at 23 Thurston Street that August, and a happy family made the best of cramped quarters. Willie carried a full course load and found a job working weekends at the local A & P Food Store. He was the master of understatement in a letter to a friend.

"I am pressed for time. It is more or less of a job to be a husband, father, college student, director of the Faith Cabin Library, and work on weekends in a grocery store."[86]

Dr. Geer was anything but understated in his comments after Buffington's freshman year.

"This young man has seized an idea and developed it. I know a great deal about what he has accomplished and I commend him and his work without reservation. It can be said of him that he not only appreciates any opportunity given him, but he sets about with industry and determination to appropriate these opportunities."[87]

Back home, Mr. Simpkins re-read the monthly letter detailing the happenings on campus, the triumphs and the adversities, and knew that his young friend was on the path for which he was destined. The farming, sawyering, and mill work were careers now brought to a close, and those doors would not re-open. The boy had accomplished much, and together he and Simpkins were still building libraries at rural crossroads and in backwoods communities. Near the end of the letter he read,

"Come to Greenville. I am preaching my ordination sermon at Pendleton Street Baptist Church on May 10th!"

Visions of broken mudpies. Long ago conversations about *Pilgrim's Progress*. Separations their friendship endured. All these came back to him. Euriah stopped and bowed his head, and after a few moments continued his walk toward the schoolhouse, singing an old hymn that filled the early spring morning.

41

Pendleton Street Baptist Church was crowded when the two men walked up to the front, escorted by the minister. Simpkins was shown to his seat of honor on the front pew as Willie continued to the podium. His sermon spoke to a life of service, of honor among friends and believers, of grace extended to all of creation. During the ordination ceremony, Mr. Simpkins was called on to speak. He graciously acknowledged his young friend's work among the poor and disadvantaged, and urged him to continue these efforts as a minister of the Gospel. Laying his hands on the boy's shoulders, he whispered, "God will provide," and hugged him. Tears came to Willie's eyes.

August, 1936: Jesse Owens wins four gold medals at the Summer Olympic Games in Berlin, Germany. He, John Woodruff, Ralph Metcalf, and Archie Williams refute Adolph Hitler's declaration of Aryan superiority.

Studies, family life and a job on weekends filled his Furman years, and yet Buffington found time to continue, and even increase, his Faith Cabin Library work. It fired the racial consciousness of journalists throughout the nation, bringing accolades from Beatrice Plumb in her December, 1935 article "Joy Bells Ringing", and from Karen Jones in May, 1937 with "Proper Setting for a Miracle." Readers took notice, and an extensive travel schedule filled with speaking engagements ensued. Students and faculty from Oberlin (OH) College heard of his work and invited him there. Buffington was overjoyed and somewhat overwhelmed that a college sophomore should lecture upperclassmen and professors on the critical subject of interracial cooperation.

From there, according to the Xenia OH *Evening Gazette*, this dynamic young man would speak at the town's First Baptist Church on Friday, August 7th; travel to Springfield (OH) to talk on Wednesday, August 12th; then wind up his tour in Dayton (OH) on Thursday, August 13th. The young people of the local Friend's Church, supporters of the Faith Cabin Libraries, made all the arrangements.[88] The *Gazette* used the story of the five 2-cent stamps, but wrongly identified the work as occurring in North Carolina. And he still wrote letters, contacting individuals and groups throughout the US and Canada. Willie once remarked that a contribution had come from Denmark.

Dr. Geer gave him full support, both as a student and in his library work.

"I regard this movement as a social enterprise of great value and I am ready to do everything I can to encourage Mr. Buffington in the promotion and enlargement of his work."[89]

Willie did not disappoint this man who made college possible. Between entering Furman in 1935 and graduating in 1938, seven additional Faith Cabin Libraries were built, stocked and staffed. The travels, speaking engagements and letters sent all over North America cultivated the necessary resources, though Euriah was always there to remind him that a dime, a dream, and faith still drove the process.

Naming the units was serious business, a duty Buffington never took lightly. The first, Lizzie Koon (Saluda), honored his birth mother; the second, Annie Bodie (Ridge Spring), did the same for his step-mother; the third, L.H. King (Newberry), spoke of the man who spearheaded the gathering of books to make the first library a reality. Collectively they started more than a movement to build libraries. For the first time in many of the rural areas of South Carolina, the opportunity existed for African-Americans to learn to read, and perchance to dream. Buffington once said of the shipments of books pouring into the state, "they must never stop; not ever".

His fourth library became the shining example for all the other locations to emulate. Miss Catherine Degen lived in New York City, read about Buffington's libraries and his work to become a minister, and gave financial assistance, both to his academic expenses and to his work.

In her letter dated February 19, 1938, the gracious support she provided was never more apparent. She sent it "with the hope that this reaches you on Monday and in good time for you and Mrs. Buffington to attend the Junior-Senior banquet." Inside was a check for $100, "twenty five for you a suit and twenty five for Mrs. Buffington a dress and shoes to go with it – the other fifty dollars to be added to your budget to cover the expense of the illness of little Ethel Margaret." Clara had written to Miss Degen after the child developed a kidney infection following a bout with tonsillitis.

Degen also supported Willie's decision to attend summer school and earn his degree in three years. Her words always precipitated action. "I shall be very glad to furnish you the funds for your summer session, and at your convenience, shall be glad to know the amount you will need to carry you through."

The libraries were never far from her mind, as she reminded him. "By the way, in October last I sent an order for the magazine (*Christian Herald*) to go to the Pendleton Unit...", and she asked that he make sure the subscription had started.[90]

This newest Faith Cabin Library was named in her honor, and when she died in 1944, her wish was that, in lieu of flowers, benevolences be sent to support the ongoing work.

Everything about the Degen unit at the Anderson County Training School in Pendleton made it unique. There was a strong, energetic and vocal board of directors. One offered the following comment:

"Young man, you have opened my eyes to the need among our Negroes, and of their eagerness to learn. From now on I promise you that I will take a more active interest in this school."[91]

It was favorably discussed in Edward Stanford's writings on the Workers Progress Administration, whose aim was to praise the WPA rather than Faith Cabin Libraries' accomplishments. He noted that this unit gave "particularly good service with very limited resources", and "is more adequate than that offered to Negroes by most communities in the state."[92] The African-American man who worked there was a WPA employee who did programs such as Book Week and Health Week. There was praise for "a popular shelf of books by Negro authors," and it became standard fare for many of the later libraries.[93]

It was the only Faith Cabin Library with screens on its doors and windows. Local teachers contributed many of the books. It housed a complete 1933 edition of Compton's Pictured Encyclopedia, and by 1940 there were 5000 books on its shelves. Many of the people who used the facility checked out and read one particular volume, *Bursting Bonds*, the autobiography of Dr. William Pickens, an African-American who was born in Pendleton. The community showed considerable interest in Negro life and history, and the hard work of the teacher/librarian, school principal and WPA librarian allowed the Catherine Degen Unit to achieve a high level of excellence.[94]

The Bessie Drew Unit in lower Greenville County began that same year at the Chapman Grove Rosenwald School, and housed 1900 books. The principal and his wife lived on site and kept the library open year round to serve the community. Drew was the managing editor of *Southern Workman*, published at the Hampton Institute (Hampton VA), and was a strong advocate of Buffington's early work (she published "An Adventure In Faith" in 1933).[95]

Willie did not forget his new friends at Oberlin College, establishing a library at Seneca Junior College in 1937 and naming it in their honor. Nor did they forget his visit to them the previous year, shipping 4000 volumes to fill the shelves. An estimated 1000 people used the facility on a regular basis.[96]

The Fountain Inn Negro School was home to the Abraham Lincoln Unit, and started operations that year. More than 4000 volumes were given by Mr. Isaac Diller (sp) of Springfield IL, the only person still living at that time to have been photographed with the heroic president. Largely because of the library, the school was chosen as the

Center for Adult Education, which local folks called "The People's College". Members of the black community supplied building materials, while the WPA furnished the construction labor and provided roofing material.[97]

Nor did Buffington forget his old friend and benefactor, Dr. Geer, naming the unit at the Rosenwald School in Belton SC after him in 1938. One of three libraries to open during Willie's senior year, it was small, and service was largely confined to the school. The 1320 volumes were donated by readers of Beatrice Plumb's December, 1935 article "Joy Bells Ringing". What made Buffington proud was the cooperation that made the unit possible.

"It is my understanding that the local Negroes, aided by some of the leading white citizens, were responsible for the materials that went into the making of the building."[98]

The Hanover-Dartmouth Unit of 1938 supported Simpson Junior High School in Easley SC, and like the Oberlin Unit, garnered most of its donations from students and college friends who heard Buffington speak during one of his fundraising tours. The local black community raised the money for building material, and a WPA grant paid for the labor to construct a shingle and board facility housing more than 3000 books. Buffington noted that "the children have become more interested in the history of their own race. Among the special needs mentioned by the principal were more books about the Negro, and books by Negro authors."[99]

The final library completed during his undergraduate years at Furman was the Iowa City Unit at Bettis Academy in Trenton SC. Much like the Catherine Degen Unit, this one held a special place in Willie's heart because it honored another old friend. He remembered the many kindnesses shown him by A.W. Nicholson, principal of the school, from listening to his dreams and offering practical advice, to designing and printing letterhead to use in his writing campaigns. People in Iowa City had read "Joy Bells Ringing", and the ministerial Association spearheaded a book drive that resulted in 9000 books shipped. Reverend Casper Garrigus, chairman of the body, said of their homegrown endeavor, "the need of the appeal was so great, the asking so modest. It impressed me as seldom I have been impressed."[100]

The building was constructed of concrete blocks made on campus, and the work was done by students and friends of the school. There was no government grant for labor. Once completed, the library was a year-round blessing, serving the school and community in the summer months as well.[101]

Ten libraries functioned as graduation day drew near, but despite the impressive achievement, Willie articulated no particular joy.

"How can I take pride in any of this? We have built ten wonderful places for people to learn, but in more than one hundred communities others have contacted me by letter, seeking libraries of their own. Each request heartfelt, each one deserving, and far more requests than we could ever honor. I can only wonder what God expects."

Simpkins traveled to graduation to deliver his answer in person. It made sense to Willie. It always did.

"The work, it's grown past what you can do by yourself, even with Clara helping you with letter writing and copying things and all. You've been a full-time student, had a family depending on you to support them, worked in a food store on Saturdays and filled in as a preacher some Sundays. Then folks ask you to do more, build one more library they say, and it will be enough. Trouble is, every letter says that."

They took another turn around campus, drawing stares and comments from some, acknowledgements and handshakes from others. Those were but momentary distractions, and Willie wanted to hear the rest. Something told him these words might be the most important he'd heard since he was Cotton Top running the red hills of Saluda.

"So tomorrow you take a degree in Social Studies, and start preparing for a move up north to that seminary. Oh my boy's gonna be a teacher, preacher, theologian and builder. Now isn't that something!" He put his arms around Willie's shoulder and hugged him. "God made the way, and will go right on doing it. Our job is to follow, do our best with what we got, help when we can, and never give up trying to pull folks along with us, make things better for them.

"These Faith Cabin Libraries, no matter if they stopped being built right now, would still make a difference. Folks been learning to read, and not just children either. They've been learning to think, and they're not afraid to dream about what might be. When Mr. Jefferson talked about all men being created equal, pursuing life and liberty and happiness, well maybe that really does mean *all* men, not just white, or rich, or somehow privileged beyond the man or woman they're standing next to."

"Things can change," the boy said.

"They *are* changing, son. And they'll change more."

"Like the libraries, it mustn't stop. It can't. It just can't."

"Nor will it. I think that's your peculiar station in life, Cotton Top." They both smiled, and Mr. Simpkins last words were buoyed by warm spring breezes as they stood at the steps of Dr. Geer's house, where he'd stay the night.

"Your grandma told you God made the miracle, and that's true. I shared with you my certainty that God would provide, and I believe that to be true as well. Now I think there's one more thing. This road you're on, it's going to get wider as the years come and go, because a lot of folks will take the way you made possible. They're going to read and think and dream. Long time ago you said it wasn't good enough to be your brother's keeper. You, we, all of us, need to be our brother's brother. All God's children. No different. Going to be a lot of people on that road, Willie. Not following, necessarily, but being there because it's the right thing to do. Doing it because we all *are* created equal, and walking that road together is the only way life can be full and complete, like it was meant to be."

Buffington watched his friend pass through the door, welcomed by Dr. and Mrs. Geer. The Furman president stepped out and shook the young man's hand as he turned to go. No need to think about sleep coming that night. Like always, Mr. Simpkins' words started him thinking.

1938: Henry Armstrong holds World Boxing Championship titles in the featherweight, welterweight and lightweight divisions.

Joe Louis avenges his 1936 loss to Max Schmeling by knocking him out in the first round to reclaim the World Boxing Heavyweight Championship.

Only Buffington could have an interesting story about a class ring. The money to buy it was a gift from his African-American friends, patrons of the libraries pooling their pennies into a generous offering. The new graduate explained that "I had the ring made the year I was a junior and thought it was going to take me four years to get out, and then went back to Hale's Jewelers with the ring which had a '39 on it. I asked if they could change that '39 to a '38. They said they could with considerable difficulty. The man said, 'I've had to change a lot of them from '29 to '30 or '35 to '36 but this is the first time I've had to set one back.'".[102]

Willie was grateful for his education at Furman, and it was obvious that he cherished his years on campus. He had certainly learned to speak up for himself when obstacles threatened to slow his library-building work, even if it involved professors and administrators.

One gentleman, Mendel S. Fletcher, insisted that the coursework in physical education should not be waived under any circumstances, even though Willie was nearing thirty years of age when he received his diploma. In a letter written after graduation and posted from Crozer Theological Seminary in August of 1938, he made his feelings known. Willie had stopped by his office at the end of summer session to speak in person, but Mr. Fletcher had left on vacation.

Acknowledging Fletcher for his interest and consideration during freshman year, Buffington minces no words in his disdain for 'PE'. "I am also anxious that you know that I never learned to appreciate the fact that YOU insisted that I be required to take the Physical Education work at Furman." He later calls it "utter nonsense (especially for a man my age)", but it was not bodily exertion, laziness, or indifference that prompted the disdain. Extraordinarily focused on the wrong he sought to right, Buffington could never brook wasting time.

"I understand that you maintained that I should be made (to) take the work for mental discipline, which is an impossibility according to the best authorities on Education. My only regret is that I could have spent many hours in a more profitable manner both to myself and to those I have sought to serve". And Willie *does* presume to lecture his elder, especially concerning his lack of compassion.

"My sincere hope is that you will act wiser next time and give some other student, maybe more deserving than I was and with more hardships, the benefit of the doubt. It is a serious matter to lay more stones in the path of a student who is already struggling with bleeding knees."

Rules were necessary to conduct activities at a university, he knew, but he did not accept that they must be unyielding. "I am confident that there are a few officials on the Furman Campus who could well afford to manifest a little more human kindness and understanding sympathy without losing any prestige. You, my dear Mr. Fletcher, may be on that list."

End of lecture. End of letter. But one cannot read the complimentary close ("With best wishes, I am, Always sincerely yours") without a smile, and without admiration for the young man so dedicated to the work he had chosen.[103]

Most of the letters Willie received asked for help in securing a library, but a very special delivery in January of 1937 asked but for a single book. Roman Koral wrote from Warsaw, Poland the year before the Nazi war machine rolled through the country.

"I read in *Reader's Digest* that you had founded libraries for your negro friends. I suppose, therefore, that You are the very person, to which I can write for help in learning English."

He told Buffington, in handwriting resembling fine calligraphy, that in the past year he taught himself German and French, and bought an English book. He read and wrote the language, but felt that further progress would be difficult because there was no money to buy a dictionary. He asked for that, or an encyclopedia, or a book about America. Perhaps recognizing a kindred spirit, Willie involved his Faith Cabin Library supporters, who gladly honored the request.[104]

Chapter 6 – Seminary and graduate school.

Undergraduate degree firmly in hand, and other libraries underway, the Buffington family made ready for another journey, their first excursion together away from South Carolina. Chester, Pennsylvania and Crozer Theological Seminary would be home for the next four years.

Three more libraries were completed in 1938, each adding a particularly inspiring story to the Faith Cabin legacy. The Albert Stamm Unit of the Inman Negro School (Inman SC) bore the name of a disabled World War I veteran who canvassed counties in northwest Ohio and northeast Indiana for donations and shipped more than 4000 volumes to eager children and adults.

The good people of Elyria OH earned the unique distinction of outfitting two libraries. Edgefield Academy (Edgefield Rosenwald School) was built with logs and stones moved by volunteers from Mose Buffington's land five miles from town, and labor was supplied through a WPA grant.[105] There was electricity, and evening hours were arranged so community patrons could peruse the 4000 volumes. Barney Dane of Elyria drove the truck, filled with books and magazines, from Ohio to South Carolina. Other precious cargo was four cabinet-sized Victrolas, two smaller Victrolas, and a radio. He returned home with a photograph of the truck being unloaded, courtesy of principal W.E. Parker.[106] Later, Mr. Parker wrote a letter of appreciation to his new friends.

"This is to advise that our library is complete and is serving a much needed cause. We want you to feel that your efforts in this direction have been time well spent. The people of this community are proud of the opportunity offered through this medium and highly appreciate what you have done for us." [107]Buffington and some older ministers met on alternate Friday evenings with six young men who planned to enter the ministry. He met with them on one occasion, and marveled at the intellectual discussion. "Why, the questions sounded like musings of 'liberals' on a college campus." [108]

The George A. Brown Unit at the Edgefield County Training School in Johnston was named for the Presbyterian minister who worked tirelessly in the Elyria community to gather the books and other items that made their way south. Buffington encouraged both Mr. Parker and Mr. Smith, principal of the Training School, to emulate the Degen Library in Pendleton. In Johnston, where each teacher had a reference shelf of books in her room, students and teachers offered special programs, and sold books and school supplies to earn money to buy works by African-American authors. At the time of Buffington's survey in 1940, they proudly showed him four newly purchased volumes. [109]

When Mr. Dayne finished unloading his cargo, the two men drove back to Greenville to load up the family belongings and head to Crozer Theological Seminary, where Buffington would begin his graduate studies that autumn. After goodbyes to Dr. and Mrs. Geer, their families, and Mr. Simpkins, they were off to Pennsylvania. Different town. Different school. Same dream. Same motto: Others.

After hurriedly moving in and getting the family somewhat settled, Willie was off to Norwich CT to pick up a 1930 Chevrolet, a gift from a Lutheran minister for the Faith Cabin work. On the way back, driving through Trenton NJ, the young man was up close and personal with a massive hurricane that wreaked havoc all along the northeastern coastline. That old car became a bit of a legend in its own right, and not just for surviving the Big Blow of '38.

One fine day, it happened to be parked outside a classroom as one professor lectured on religious philosophy. Seizing the moment, he pointed to the car and pronounced it a stellar example of illusion in Plato's theory of ideal forms. Drowsy and otherwise distracted students were suddenly wide awake, and dubbed the old jalopy "Buffington's Pile of Philosophical Junk." [110] The name stuck, and the old car served the man and his work faithfully for many years, and made its way back to South Carolina before being retired from active duty.

Willie went New York City to appear on Dave Elman's "Hobby Lobby" radio show. Guests were invited because of their unusual interests, and for Elman, this bespectacled young man's efforts to build libraries for his brothers and sisters crossed over into inspiration. Listeners contributed more than 4500 books, and in 1940 the Hobby Lobby Unit opened at the Lexington SC Negro School. Since the building had electricity, Mr. Elman donated an expensive radio for use. Children and adults alike enjoyed it, but especially the older people who could not read. One of the teachers, Martha Wright, praised the efforts.

"Children are already book conscious, even in this short time. They are learning to utilize their spare time in reading for pleasure." [111]

It was much more than a hobby, much more than an avocation or a good deed rendered for a short while. The books, and the knowledge they held, became the very life blood for people long denied the chance to learn. Though hundreds of miles away from home, Buffington never allowed the work to stop.

As he always did, Willie studied long and hard. Two of his term papers during those years showed how deeply he was plumbing the depths of his calling to set right grievous wrongs. "The Person of Jesus: Historically Considered and Evaluated From a Modern Viewpoint", was written in May, 1940, and "The Work of Christ (The Atonement)" followed in November, 1941. His Christian Theology professors had no concerns about the young man's critical thought. He also worked hard to provide living expenses for his family. During the first three years at seminary, he was the director of religious education at the 5th Presbyterian Church, a black congregation. His last year, he pastored a small Baptist church Sunday mornings and evenings. And he was a handyman, finding yards to mow, picking up additional money to keep the wolves away from the door.

"It's hard, I know it is, boy. Most things worthwhile, they stay hard, that's just the way the world is. There isn't much money, but you still provide for the missus and those two chaps. Nobody's hungry yet." He felt the cadence of his friend's words as if they were face to face in the fields back home, sweating under a summer sun to finish a repair job on one of the libraries. Willie smiled, even through his worry.

"You always get that big grin when I say 'God will provide', and I know you're doing it now" – he was right – "but the Lord's looking out after you, just like he's looking after those sparrows that surely must fly around the Crozer grounds. Lots of prayers go up all day long from your old friend down in South Carolina. He doesn't forget you, and he believes in you, in all the good things you're doing and are going to do in the future. Take this little bit of money to ease things for your family, Willie Lee. Write when you can, in the midst of all that studying, husbanding, fathering and library building. Your daddy lets me know when another load of books comes in and where they are going. God's still making miracles, isn't he?

"Your Friend, Euriah"

Willie held the three crumpled dollars in his hands and wept. There would be no giving up. Not before. Not now. Not ever. There just wasn't any way he would ever fail Mr. Simpkins, nor all those souls who found sanctuary inside the walls of the libraries.

1939: *Way Down South*, by Langston Hughes, debuted. The interracial movie stars Clarence Muse.

Easter Sunday, 1939: Opera singer Marian Anderson is refused permission to enter Constitution Hall by the Daughters of the American Revolution. At the insistence of Secretary of the Interior Harold Ickes, she instead performs in front of the Lincoln Memorial before an integrated crowd of 75,000.

1939: In New York City, Billie Holliday first performs "Strange Fruit" a song protesting lynching.

Names of the units established while he was at Crozer were often unfamiliar references to individual donors, groups or communities. The number of those founded (fourteen in addition to Hobby Lobby) matched those names with equally endearing stories of people who cared. The Decatur Unit at the Batesburg South Carolina Negro School (1939) held 3500 volumes from Decatur, Indiana, collected by Mrs. S.D. Beavers. She was inspired by Beatrice Plumb's "Joy Bells Ringing" in the December, 1935 *Christian Herald*, and wanted only to share in Buffington's work. The Saluda Rosenwald School welcomed 3100 books housed in the Mt. Gretna Unit (1940). Margaret Mansfield organized donations through this Pennsylvania drama company, and appeals were made from the stage as they began their 1937 summer stock. When WPA workers completed the building's foundation, they left and did not return, so Principal Harrison J. Trapp and an unnamed agricultural teacher supervised the older school boys and completed the building.[112] The Lucy Harris Unit at the Howard School in Georgetown SC (1940) received 2100 volumes from listeners of the Hobby Lobby radio broadcast and from readers of Plumb's articles. Euriah Simpkins finally agreed to lend his name to the unit at the Bouknight School in Johnston SC (1940), where 2000 volumes came from the same audiences. Jamestown NY citizens were reached in like manner and provided 2100 books to the Jamestown Unit (1940), on site at the Jamestown Negro School in their South Carolina sister city.

1940: Richard Wright's *Native Son* is published.

February, 1940: Hattie McDaniel is the first African American to win a Motion Picture Academy Award, claiming Best Supporting Actress for her role as Mammy in *Gone With The Wind*.

January, 1941: The US Army forms the combat unit known as the Tuskegee Airmen.

June, 1941: President Franklin D. Roosevelt issues Executive Order 8802, the Fair Employment Act, requiring equal treatment of all employees by defense contractors.

In his first year at Crozer, Buffington was invited by Reverend Earle Edwards of the Queens Village (NY) Baptist Church to talk about the libraries. With the slogan "10,000 Books in 10 Weeks", Edwards invited the entire community for the evening lecture. They met that goal, effectively creating the Queens Village Unit at the Marlboro Training School in Bennettsville SC in 1941. On a trip back from Florida to New York, the good reverend stopped by for a visit, and later wrote to Buffington.

"A grand job that fellow Wright (the principal who loaned books to 15 other black schools in the county) is doing. We are happy that we could have a small part in it."[113]

The Rockford Unit at the Aiken SC Negro School opened that same year and housed 2000 volumes for local citizens. It was made possible through the work of Mrs. Oscar Hall and the generosity of the Illinois town's Lutheran churches.

Willie named one of the libraries after his father, only fair since Daddy did most of the receiving, packaging and shipping of books after his son matriculated north for his graduate studies. The M.W. Buffington Unit was founded at the Elisha Rosenwald Community School in Silverstreet SC in 1941, housed 1700 books, and through the leadership of Principal A.F. Butler, was built without the aid of public funds. A bittersweet story survives as the legacy of this unit.

"One of the Elisha School graduates uses the library extensively," Buffington reported, "though she is unable to continue her high school career due to the distance to the Drayton Street High School",[114] in the town of Newberry some eight miles away. This was the second Faith Cabin Library in the county, soon to be joined by a unit at the Whitmire Negro School (1200 volumes) and the Leitzsey Unit at the school of the same name in the Mt. Bethel Community (1800 volumes).

One library had the distinction of residing in the city of Greenville, a most non-rural location long known as the Textile Capital of the World in honor of its many cotton mills. Mrs. Mary Ross Collins, Professor of Speech at Crozer, persuaded the Musical Matinee Club of Philadelphia PA to sponsor the Harry A. Mackey Unit at Sterling High School. The 3200 volumes arriving in 1941 effectively tripled the size of the existing library.[115] The Doolittle-Howe Unit, Mt. Carmel Rosenwald School in the Owens Community of McCormick County SC (2900 volumes, 1942); Swarthmore Unit, Gray Court Negro School, Laurens County SC (2200 volumes coming from the young people of a church in Swarthmore PA, 1942); and the unit at Chesnee SC Negro School (1200 volumes, 1942) rounded out Buffington's extracurricular work while at seminary.

He now replied to donors with a short card containing a poem he had written, titled "We Thank You!"

Just how much you help us/ You can never know.
Blessed are the helpers/ Everywhere they go.
Here's a bit of gratitude/ Going straight to you.
Heartily we say it/ And Jesus says it too. [116]

A three page summary concluded his survey of libraries completed by 1940, and Buffington offered this understatement of the accomplishment. "Practically every official that I have contacted during this survey commented about the increase in interest among the youth in books and reading, and books are items of luxury to the masses of Negroes and many whites in the South…The enthusiasm manifested by some of the young people I met and talked with, not to speak of the things related by teachers and principals, encourage me."[117]

In his own way, Buffington sowed seeds that blossomed during the Civil Rights movement of the 1950's and 1960's. His many African American friends read, talked, debated, and shared books and knowledge. Learning to read cost Jim Crow several thousand field hands, and the education that resulted led them to re-examine and eventually claim Thomas Jefferson's words that all people were indeed created equal.

By 1942, Willie found a way to simultaneously earn degrees from two institutions. Dr. James H. Franklin, president of the seminary, allowed Buffington to use twelve semester hours he earned at the University of Pennsylvania to fulfill requirements for his Bachelor of Divinity degree. The university reciprocated, allowing a like number of hours earned at Crozer to apply toward a Master of Arts degree. There was a wonderful added bonus to all this. Euriah Simpkins came to watch Willie graduate, courtesy of Franklin and some friends who footed travel expenses, and was presented with an honorary Bachelor of Arts degree at the graduation ceremony.[118]

"It was a great day in the old gentleman's life," Willie was fond of saying.

Chapter 7 – Can anybody make a difference in a world like this?"

The winter of 1942 found Buffington completing his academic work, preparing for final exams, and looking to the future. For years, he never believed he could get even a high school education, but he did that and went on to college. Now, he was on the threshold of two advanced degrees, and all he could focus on was the question pounding in his head. What next?

"God's provided, Euriah, but now I don't know. A big world, most of it at war, young people, black and white, marching off to fight against evil, and yet we got so much evil right here at home, especially in the south. And when our Negro friends come back after winning this conflict, and we must believe that will happen, they're going to find exactly what they left. Jim Crow. Segregation. Poverty.

"Can anybody make a difference in a world like this?"

The answer wasn't long coming. Lots of news about boys home on furlough before shipping out. Lots of news about boys who wouldn't be coming back to the cool waters of Red Bank Creek. Then the last few simple words, a precise and even presence on the page.

"God's still providing. He always will."

Willie wrote to Channing Tobias in February, filling him in on the books coming from Grand Rapids MI in an ongoing response to the Hobby Lobby Radio Show, letting him know of the Bachelor of Divinity and Master of Arts degrees coming in June. He signed off with,

"I am busy these days. Pardon the card."[119]

In a quick reply, his old friend offered some employment advice to the soon-to-be-graduate.

"I have always thought of you in connection with work there (at Paine College) and believe that you would be able to render a most acceptable service."[120]

The same evening Willie received Tobias' letter, he sat quietly at the kitchen table and answered. Blackout shades were down, the children were tucked into bed, and even Clara had retired early. Lighting a stubby candle, he drew out two sheets of FCL letterhead, Crozer Theological Seminary version.

"I wish to say that I have already taken the matter up with Dr. Peters, and while he has not said it would be impossible to find a place for me, he has frankly advised that I not depend too heavily upon it. This amounts to about the same thing that I have received from the Southern Baptist Mission Board.

56

"My struggle has been so severe that I become impatient when it seems that there will be no place for me. It is not about what I have prepared for, but in a last resort I can turn to the Army as a chaplain."

He paused for a bit, rubbed his tired eyes, and added one last paragraph.

"I would like to enter a pastorate in the South but I also want to carry on the library work, and I fear difficulties would arise...certainly, unless I had a liberal congregation, and after careful consideration of all the factors...the best work can be done in connection with a school like Paine."[121]

Just as Buffington secured a strong ally in Dr. B.E. Geer while at Furman, he did likewise with Dr. James H. Franklin at Crozer. The seminary leader contacted the Missionary Board of the Southern Baptist Convention to let them know that his charge was very interested in interracial work. A job interview resulted.

"I was invited by Dr. John Jacob Starkes of Benedict College to come and talk about a job. And I traveled (to Columbia SC) at the college's expense."[122] Interestingly, Starkes had been the first president of the Seneca Institute (and Junior College) in Seneca SC years before Buffington established the Oberlin Unit of the Faith Cabin Library there in 1937. (NOTE: That library building still stands, though all other buildings were razed in 1963).The interview went well enough to excite the young man, and he returned to Crozer, energized to wrap up his studies in a blaze of glory.

After graduation, with no word from Dr. Starkes, Willie found work at the Chester shipyard. He wasn't an Army chaplain, but did contribute to the national defense through his work that summer. One hot evening late in July he returned home, worn out from the day's work. Willie Jr. and little Ethel Margaret greeted him as he walked through the yard. Hugging them tightly, he looked up to see Clara, standing barefoot on the front steps. Her smile gave it all away.

"The letter, it came, and oh Willie, I opened it. Please forgive me. I..."

"Benedict?"

"We're going home!" She giggled, running to him and taking her turn at a kiss and a bear hug.

He arrived too late to have his name and teaching duties printed in the Benedict Bulletin for the 1942-43 academic year, and described his arrival in a letter to friends on Faith Cabin Library letterhead sporting the college's name and address.

"Greetings from South Carolina! You cannot imagine the joy that is ours in being able to inform you of our change of address…My duties here at Benedict will consist of teaching in the college and theological departments, and during the summer months I shall be engaged in a program of education and training of Negro ministers who have not had opportunity for college and seminary training." He closes the letter, "Yours for a better world."[123]

Dr. Starkes, the man who hired Buffington and found the family their home on South Walker Street, was the first African-American president of the school, begun in 1870 for recently emancipated slaves, and chartered as a liberal arts college by the state legislature in 1894. There were no complaints about the new employee's teaching ability and enthusiasm for the job.

He emerged from his work at the end of the first semester, pausing long enough to write a letter to Dr. Tobias during the Christmas break.

"I am happy in my work and have been given a royal welcome by both faculty and students at Benedict…During the State Baptist Convention here in the First Baptist Church recently, I was given 6 minutes in which to make an appeal to South Carolina Baptists to take more seriously their opportunities for cooperation with Negro Baptists."[124]

Always profoundly grateful to Tobias, his final paragraph acknowledged just how much he owed the man.

"Your interest and support during the years of struggle for education was as a great tonic…If I can ever do anything to repay you please call upon me. I shall be busy during the summer holding Institutes for Negro ministers, but if I can serve you or the Y.M.C.A in any small way I shall make a special effort to serve."[125]

It was not entirely to be sociable and informative that he wrote his old friend and benefactor. The Phelps-Stokes Fund, which provided vocational and technical education for African-Americans and Native Americans, and which supported the Jeanes Teacher program (a model for education in the rural south), awarded Buffington a grant to help pay his own school expenses. He asked Tobias whether this might be extended and used to carry on the Faith Cabin Library work.

Tobias, never one to sit and wait for things to happen – he was serving as an advisor to the Fund at this time – wrote back almost immediately.

"As I recall, the appropriations decided upon at our meeting of the Phelps-Stokes Board last month, there is an item for Faith Cabin Libraries."[126]

His parting words were warm. "With every good wish, and trusting that you will feel free to write me frequently..." [127]

1943: Dr. Charles P. Drew is the first African-American surgeon to serve as an examiner on the American Board of Surgery.

1943: Race riots erupt in Detroit, Michigan.

The library work did not stop even as he moved his family back home and began his teaching career. In November, he wrote letters acknowledging receipt of more than 100 parcels and shipments of books. Volumes were placed in the Starkes School of Theology at Benedict, and two new library units were opened at Camp Liberty (Jenkinsville) and New Bethel High School (Spartanburg). Plans were made to establish a unit at Friendship College in Rock Hill, but transportation problems associated with war-time gas rationing prevented the shipment from leaving Edgefield. [128] Buffington made no further mention that this particular endeavor was successful.

People still wrote about this white southerner building libraries for his black neighbors. Ann Murchison called him a teacher-missionary, having "the privilege of working with young men and women – building character and strengthening the bonds of Christian fellowship."[129] In an American Baptist publication, Willie Lee talked about what building the libraries had achieved, noting that "the results of the first ten years of the original Faith Cabin Libraries are to be discussed in the community as you probe for them, not as you look over the columns of a balance sheet."[130]

April 3, 1944: In Smith vs. Albright, the US Supreme Court determines the whites-only Democratic Party primary in Texas is unconstitutional.

Edward Stanford, author of the study of the Works Progress Administration (WPA) efforts in library extension, and who had earlier praised the Pendleton Faith Cabin library, nonetheless decried the "poor collection of books" in most other locations. He was writing for the benefit of the New Deal Program, part of President Franklin Roosevelt's vital economic package for America during the Great Depression, so the

Faith Cabin Library, Pendleton SC. Rear view.
The building remains standing.
Photo taken by author.

Faith Cabin Library, Pendleton SC. The gentleman is Robert Thompson, who graduated from the nearby Anderson County Training School in 1943, and remembers spending hours in the Catherine Degen Unit, "lined to the rafters with books." The day we walked through the building, we could find no trace of the motto, Others. "Rest assured, it was there," he said. Thompson went on to graduate from South Carolina State University, and eventually returned to Pendleton to live, work, marry, raise a family, and serve as a city councilman as well.

Photo taken by author.

objects of his praise were not surprising.[131] The "poor collections", however, were windows to a bigger world where the readers were determined to take their rightful places and earn a better life for themselves and their race. Those joy bells, heard by only a few that day in Plum Branch when the first library opened its doors, were beginning to ring loudly.

"We both watched it, those years when news of lynchings filled the local papers, and fear ruled everything. Evil moved from the street to the heart, and there didn't seem to be an end in sight. But then the books started coming, black people learned to read, and somehow love got added to intelligence and trust."

His fingers caressed the piece of paper like it was a treasure of great value.

"It was a love that kept my people standing, made them feel there was goodness and hope, that the darkness and despair could be overcome. You gave that to them, boy, remember it always. You gave that to them."

Willie had the entire letter from back in 1935, when he left for Furman, but this page he kept carefully folded in his wallet. When things got confusing, or lonely, or just plain hard, the wisdom of Euriah Simpkins was the balm of Gilead. There was shelter from the storm in his simple words.

The young man worried about his friend these days. Mose Buffington kept his son informed about Simpkins' health. "Since he lost his beloved Martha, it's harder for him, son." They talked of it on Willie's trips to Edgefield to pack up loads of books for new libraries. "Man loses his helpmate, sometimes loneliness sets in, and he marks the days until they can be together again, lying side by side in the earth, walking side by side in the presence of God."

It was almost Christmas, 1943, a good three months since he had written to his friend. A busy semester, full of classes and filling in as a preacher at local churches on Sundays, of helping Clara at home with Willie Jr. and Ethel Margaret, of too many bills and too little money. Days filled with news of war. It was cold and rainy. Exams were graded and stacked on the hall table. He rested in his chair by the fire, and it was after eleven when he started the letter.

He wrote, and scenes flashed before him, twisting paths of transition begun when he first heard the words, "Be a man. The world needs men."

"You gave me everything, made something useful from what most folks considered little more than trash. I owe you so much more than I could ever repay, and here, this evening, in the solitude of night, I acknowledge all that you are to me."

He talked on for three more pages, about the children, Clara, his dad. He shared classroom successes and the travails of a rookie teacher, and how the library work was really what he wanted to do. The last sentence, when he finished and re-read the words, seemed almost from some ancient literature.

"Of all I have learned, this is the most important you ever imparted to me: I am not my mistakes or my regrets. I am the smile on the face of the boy or girl who realized a dream because I cared."

It was the only time he signed, "With All My Love."

Euriah's reply came New Year's Eve. The strong, meticulous strokes were shaky now. Not weak, but betraying an unsteady hand. His words still carried the laughter of the boy within, the hope of the consummate dreamer who refused to entertain the possibility that dreams might fail to materialize.

"Sometimes you think you haven't made the difference you should have, and that's not all bad, Willie Lee. Drives you on, makes you think what you've been seeking just hasn't been found yet. But understand this, you find your way when it's right, when you look for that one thing you might yet do that's going help folks the most.

"What's going to last until heaven, boy? I ask myself that a lot these days. Answer's always the same. How deep we loved. How much we were willing to give to help those who could hardly get up off the hard ground. I have been proud of you many times, but never so much as when you talked at the library opening in Plum Branch. Remember? 'Let me not be my brother's keeper. Let me be my brother's brother.' You had to rise above the storm and deceit of this life to understand that.

"Always love you too, boy. You have been my own flesh and blood. Can't any man, daddy, brother, or friend ever mean more to me. Kindred spirits, brothers like only God could make us. Nobody could love you more."

Some weeks later, tears splashed onto the sleeve of Willie's carefully pressed suit, his only one, black and always fitting him like he was the best dressed preacher there ever was, thanks to Clara's unending alterations. It would be just him making the libraries work now. Euriah was gone, already holding hands with his lovely Martha, walking along those streets where hate and poverty and prejudice didn't exist. Folks from across the countryside walked to the funeral. Blacks and whites came to pay tribute to the humble school teacher whose exemplary life bound them all together.

'God will make a way'. The young man didn't know if was his own whisper, or one filtering down from heaven.

There had been many sleepless nights the previous years, and Willie expected that a few more wouldn't matter as he sorted out in his mind just where he was supposed to be. For whatever reasons, his work at Benedict left him unfulfilled, and the library work suffered as well. No new ones had been founded since New Bethel in Spartanburg County SC in 1943. Buffington heard once more Channing Tobias saying "I always thought of you at Paine."

He slipped on his coat and locked the back door behind him. Winter stars shone in a clear, moonless sky as he ambled back and forth across campus and returned home after 2:00 AM.

"We should talk," Clara said, waiting for him in the kitchen. She handed him a cup of coffee as he preferred, no sugar or cream.

"How can I do this without him?"

"There are three great truths I believe you've been blessed with, Willie Lee. First, Uncle Eury always said that God will provide, and heaven knows we've seen that again and again in our life together. Second, your grandmother taught you that He makes the miracle. And third, I've been by your side, and like those first two, that doesn't change. Not now, not ever. I'll help with the work, too."

"You always have." He kissed and held her in the silence and the darkness. They awoke rested and resolute. Willie contacted Dr. Peters by phone, and details came together for the move to Augusta.

"Dr. Starkes, will understand," Clara called after him on his way out the door.

Buffington's life was best detailed in his correspondence with those who helped move the work of the libraries forward, as with Dr. Channing Tobias and Dr. Will Alexander. Such was the case in his exchange of letters, beginning in August, 1944, with Una Roberts Lawrence, a most fascinating woman.

Within the Southern Baptist Convention, she worked for both the Women's Missionary Union (WMU) and the Home Mission Board, and still found time to author ten books on the lives and accomplishments of Baptist missionaries. The bulk of her efforts (1926-1947) came as the Study Editor for all literature the Board circulated to churches and their members. She was involved with the work of black Baptist churches, and shared at least some of Willie's passion for helping the African-American community.

Willie submitted his resignation to Dr. Starkes and the Home Mission Board on June 1, 1944, to be effective August 31st. His first letter, obviously a response to Lawrence, came on August 4th.

"I heartily agree that our young people's organizations are missing a great opportunity for practical, effective Christian service here at home when they overlook the great need among our Negro people."[132]

Buffington struggled with the decision to leave Benedict, of that there was little doubt. The balance between his livelihood (teaching) and his passion (Faith Cabin Libraries) was always a delicate one, and he fought to make certain the library work did not suffer. Lawrence was sympathetic to his struggle. Her answer on August 12th was lengthy as she implored him to remain in Columbia.

"Everyone greatly regrets you leaving our work," she said, and quickly followed with a plea. "I hope that the leadership of the Holy Spirit will be so plain in you, that you will soon find it possible to be back with us, as we need you very much." A few sentences later, she added a gentle admonition, "But you belong with your own Baptist folk! And we need you!"[133]

They were not strangers to one another, having met the summer before at Ridgecrest, the Baptist Assembly located in the Blue Ridge Mountains of western North Carolina. Willie respected her dedication and heart for missions, and she reciprocated, acknowledging his kindred spirit of service anchored by an iron resolve. Though she had spoken of his remaining at Benedict, Una knew that Willie's word was his bond, and his eyes were resolutely set on another destination.

"Even at Paine, I can see no reason why our Baptist young people should not line up with you in the work of the Faith Log Cabin libraries. I do not know just how we should act to 'get in' on this work," though she envisioned "thousands of youngsters who would eagerly become collectors of books."[134]

Buffington's response on August 20th was both courteous and confessional. He thanked her for her dedication to the library work. "I appreciate your keen interest and sincerely hope you can do something to interest young people in collecting and sending books for this project."[135]

But he spent much of the letter sharing what had transpired. "I sometimes wonder now if anyone knows the position I faced this past summer in trying to execute planned institutes without funds." He agonized over what had to be done. "No one has deeper regrets about the whole affair than I do. I prayed about it for weeks…It was the hardest part of the decision – to say 'yes' in the face of the Negro ministers studying at Benedict."[136]

"I suppose," he continued, with sentiments that would surface again in a few years, "they all felt that I was just a chronic complainer and that all would work out – and I think it did. I had no desire to make a change if I could have been assured that I could have continued at Benedict, with freedom to plan and execute work for and with Negroes".[137] Una learned that he has not only taken a pay cut to go to Paine, but also paid his own moving expenses to get there.

She took the time to understand how difficult the whole episode was, and how deeply it affected him. Supporting Buffington to the fullest, she complimented his work, knowing that his programs would continue in his absence. "The work you have done at Benedict…both as a teacher and in the Institutes has been of such a high order and so completely satisfactory that we feel it can be well used as a pattern, even if we must now look for another to continue it."[138]

Buffington arranged to finish the summer session at Benedict, fulfilling his contract. His young men and women offered encouragement, hugs and tears, as did Dr. Starkes. Now it was on to Paine, founded in 1882 by the Methodist Episcopal Church South, gaining college status in 1903 and boasting an interracial and international faculty.

The move was based in part on the fact that Faith Cabin Libraries would be integral to his new job. Not only would there be the opportunity to make contributions to race relations, but the library work would be a major outreach of the college. Twenty nine units functioned in South Carolina, and he spent time writing letters to make sure those beacons of hope operated efficiently. Buffington taught a full schedule that first year, "so heavy until I could not get away from the campus to do any field work."[139] His classes were Tuesdays, Thursdays and Saturdays, so extended trips were not possible. He and Clara continued to handle the administrative duties associated with the libraries despite busy days in the classroom and chasing after two children. Those were happy times, doing what they felt was important work, and striving hard to make a difference. By the second year, however, ill winds began to stir.

Buffington was paid $2400 annually at Benedict, with housing included. He was told that Paine had a salary scale favorable to those with teaching experience in college, but this proved not to be the case when a colleague lacking such credentials was paid the same. And he had to pay rent for a house. Secondly, he elected to be paid in twelve monthly increments rather than nine, since expenses continued through the summer. He was then asked to teach summer school.

"With simple trust, I said 'yes'".

He initially received no compensation for the extra duties, and when he inquired, was told that his was a twelve month contract, and that he was due no other pay. After further objections, he was finally awarded $150 for the six weeks of work.[140]

1945: The Freeman Field Mutiny (Freeman Army Airfield, Seymour IN) occurs as black officers attempt to desegregate an all-white officers' club.

The following year, his on-campus duties increased, and found him serving as chairman of the Religious Life and Work Committee. This involved Wednesday evening meetings of the Epworth League, teaching Sunday School, working with students on worship programs, and securing speakers for Sunday evening vespers.[141] He also served as part of Paine's Rural Community Project, and used the Faith Cabin Library station wagon for this purpose.

Days filled with on-campus commitments left little time for building libraries, though that work never stopped. Paine's agreement to take on the library sponsorship meant much in moving the program forward, but that progress was not fast enough for Buffington. He spoke often of the workload, "...the long hours of writing letters, unpacking and assorting books. Our responsibilities have been entirely too heavy. It does not seem to be good common sense or good religion to attempt more than one can do without some sense of satisfaction."[142]

1946: Renaissance man and legendary theater performer Paul Robeson founds the American Crusade Against Lynching.

During his second year, the school increased the budget enough to pay Mrs. Buffington $600 per year (her first ever wages since their work began in earnest in 1931) and fund part-time hours for two students. There was an overwhelming sense of urgency settling upon Buffington, leaving little room for patience or understanding when the library work was not at full throttle. More money was available than ever before, but he complained that the electricity used in his garage where books were handled was part of his monthly utility bill. "The administration has refused to make any arrangements for this," was his response.[143]

Something harsh and very real drove him. Perhaps it was the death of Mr. Simpkins; perhaps the realization that he was almost 40 years old and time may have begun to run out; perhaps that African-American war veterans, returning from defending the world against

67

fascism and Nazi hatred, were expected to resume their status as second class citizens in their own country. One thing, however, was certain. Whatever the disagreements between Buffington and the college administration, more people than ever before were taking notice of the libraries and the people they served.

Buffington never tired of teaching young people on either side of the racial divide. In his continuing correspondence with Una Roberts Lawrence, he set forth his ideas on life in the newly birthed Atomic Age.

"Our scientific civilization," he told students, "has made a once large world into a neighborhood – a whispering gallery. Our Lord, in his Gospel, would have us – his disciples - take this community of peoples and make of it a brotherhood. Except we do this – in an age of atomic power – we shall perish. I can best be a brother to my brother by seeing him as a person."[144]

In that "whispering gallery", one heard again the motto over the door of the first library: Others. He continued his words of wisdom to this younger generation frightened by what it had witnessed at Hiroshima and Nagasaki.

"With a Universal God, loving and caring for all men, let us meet the conditions for discipleship and build that brotherhood that is the kingdom of God here in our world. Then no man shall need fear the recently harnessed force of the atom."

Rather than giving in to despair, he encouraged them to embrace a future filled with promise. "Follow the spirit of Christ in the matter of dealing with your fellow man - whether he be Japanese, Negro, Mexican, Indian, African or what have you – and you will be building for a new and better day."[145] The country boy from Saluda moved quite comfortably on the world stage.

His work always appealed to people, and he was sought out by writers and journalists. Three media events occurred from 1946 to 1948 that accelerated Faith Cabin Library work almost beyond what could be handled. Betty Burleigh penned "Libraries In Cabins" for *World Outlook* in March, 1946, a straightforward narrative from Buffington's first letter writing campaign, through his personal education achievements, to his successes in bringing books to African-American communities throughout South Carolina. She described him "of medium build, on the heavy side, and often smooths his hand over his dark brown hair,"[146] but highlighted beyond any doubt his humility and generosity toward others.

"The credit is not mine, for it's just as the old Negro woman (Simpkins' sister) said, 'We had nothing to go on but faith.' That's what built them all, faith, hard work, and the generosity of thousands of people willing to share their books."[147]

Photos of Buffington and Euriah Simpkins together, and of the South Carolina libraries at Plum Branch (Saluda), Bettis Academy (Trenton) Seneca, Belton, Easley, and Lexington spoke to the enormity of the effort in motion, and gave Burleigh the perfect service-oriented conclusion to her article.

Herman Styler's "He Worked Wonders With Faith And A Dime" appeared in the June, 1947 issue of *Coronet* and continued to fuel the movement. Buffington, he wrote, "did practical good in a disordered world. His was a journey into enlightened democracy, and a step toward a stronger (and better) nation."[148] His readers, like Burleigh's, came through with thousands of books, and the article also laid the groundwork for another "first". When Buffington wrote to the New York Methodist Women's Conference in October of 1947, it marked the first time he solicited donations for anything other than books and postage. He asked for friends to buy "a little all-steel bodied Jeep Station Wagon to replace his old 1930 "philosophical pile of junk" Chevrolet, which was now a mechanical pile of junk as well. His effort was successful, and $700 of the necessary $1800 was collected. He also informed the Conference of the library they funded in Dublin, Georgia, housed within the local Negro High School.

"The new flower in the garden of libraries is yours. It is set down in the midst of fertile soil and has great possibilities."[149]

April 15th, 1947: Jackie Robinson is in the Brooklyn Dodgers line-up at Ebbets Field on Opening Day against the Boston Braves. He is the first African-American to play major league baseball in the 20th century.

1947: Columbia SC entrepreneur George Elmore challenges the state's all-white Democratic Party Primary. The court victory, Elmore vs. Rice, results in thousands of African-Americans casting ballots the next year. Elmore paid dearly, losing his home and business in a white economic backlash, and dying a pauper in 1959.

May 12-21, 1947: Willie Earle is murdered in Greenville SC. Accused of assaulting and killing a white cab driver, he is lynched by a mob of 31 white men (28 cab drivers). The trial, which results in acquittal of all defendants, draws national attention and widespread outrage, and spurs new federal civil rights efforts.

July 12ᵗʰ, 1948: At the Democratic National Convention, Senator Hubert Humphrey delivers a controversial speech in favor of civil rights.

July 26ᵗʰ, 1948: President Harry S. Truman signs Executive Order 9981, desegregating the United States Armed Forces. "It is hereby declared to be the policy of the President that there shall be equality of treatment and opportunity for all persons in the armed services without regard to race, color, religion or national origin."

Styler's article launched the third media event, when Faith Cabin Libraries were the subject of a broadcast on the Ted Malone Radio Show. Sponsored by the Westinghouse Electric Corporation of Pittsburgh PA, Malone, known as "your Westinghouse storyteller", was a household name due to his renown as a World War II correspondent. He read Styler's work, and had his assistant correspond with Buffington in the spring of 1948, not only to do the show, but also to have the show sponsor a library unit. They wanted to make it a memorial to an as-yet unnamed community's war dead, Jessie Wiley Voils explained, where "the story of one boy could be told." She commended Buffington, noting what a touch of faith might accomplish. "Well, faith is contagious, or at least your kind of faith is."[150] Buffington remained adamant that the libraries were the only things that mattered, not his efforts. "The only excuse for publicity of this work is that it may help others to a better understanding of our mutual problems of living together and helping others to a fuller life."[151]

Westinghouse Presents aired Malone's broadcast on October 6ᵗʰ, 1948, and he brought it off beautifully. "Seems impossible...46 libraries started with a dime, but Willie Buffington has done it...he really has...and it proves what we're always saying, that you can do anything you want to do, if you'll just make up your mind what you want...and then do it."[152]

People read and listened to this ongoing phenomenon of the Faith Cabin Library movement, and there could be no doubt of its growing impact. During this time, ten different Methodist Women's Society conferences gave between 3000 and 10,000 useable books.[153]

With all of the support the library work received from women's groups, it may have surprised supporters that the work's primary adversary was a woman. Estellene Walker, Executive Secretary of the South Carolina State Library Board, began an exchange of letters with Buffington in November and December of 1947, who by this time had been teaching at Paine College and establishing libraries in Georgia for

70

almost three years. Her first letter began with a tone best described as condescending.

"We have been curious recently to see these libraries mentioned several times in various periodicals. As the state agency immediately concerned with library extension, we feel that we should be in possession of the facts concerning these libraries."[154]

Whether she saw this as territorial intrusion, or an overt confrontation about providing access to books for fully half of the state's population, or a mixture of the two, has been obscured by the passing of almost seventy years. Her letter continued with a narrative of the activities of the State Board. "As you doubtless know, the state of South Carolina has been interested in library extension for a long time.

"We are particularly interested in seeing library services extended to negroes," citing county-wide service in Anderson, Pickens, Greenville, Cherokee, Lancaster, Darlington, Richland (which she types twice) and Orangeburg. She followed this with mentions of city-wide service in Spartanburg, Aiken, Kershaw, Sumter, Florence and Charleston. Charleston was her shining star "for outstanding service for the entire population of the county."[155]

Faith Cabin Libraries began in 1931. Why did it take sixteen years for officials in South Carolina to notice Buffington's efforts if they were offering such stellar service to African-Americans? By then the architect was continuing his work in Georgia.

Willie carefully measured his words and crafted a response on December 18th. He was both polite and coldly factual, and little could have been misinterpreted. As she listed the areas of "service" to the black communities, he listed functioning libraries providing the treasures of books and education to children and adults: the two in Saluda County; Drayton Street School in Newberry; the Anderson County Training School in Pendleton; Easley; Belton; Fountain Inn; Gray Court; Bennettsville; Georgetown; Bettis Academy; and Edgefield. He detailed for her how these libraries operated. Collections of books offered to the communities (primarily through the schools located there) numbered from 2000-10,000; when the building was completed, books were sent and a local teacher doubled as the librarian, usually under his supervision. Buffington's closing paragraph underscored the work involved.

"Of course, you need to know that I am a full-time worker at Paine College and all the details in connection with receiving, assorting and acknowledging the books that make up these collections must be done in spare time as a labor of love."[156] Reading between the lines, his passion flowed: I'm doing this because no one else cared enough, and it is the right thing to do.

1950: Dr. Ralph Bunche wins the Nobel Peace Prize.

October 6th, 1950: Willie Buffington speaks at the NAACP meeting in Aiken SC.

There seemed to have been no response to Buffington's letter, but Walker offered comments in her later correspondence to others. The *Charleston News and Courier* (February, 1951) quoted her as dismissing the Faith Cabin Library volunteer movement as part of history in South Carolina.[157] The next year, she responded to a letter from Biloxi MS resident Amanda Love, who sought to assist Buffington's work with a donation.

"...so far as I know, there are no active Faith Cabin Libraries in South Carolina. Service to Negro residents is given through the regular library systems."[158]

1951: The South Carolina State Legislature creates what is known as the Gressette Committee to stall integration. One of their recommendations is to end compulsory education.

Walker, whose tenure with the State Library Board spanned the years 1946-1979, penned a history of South Carolina libraries a year after she retired. In the section "The Public Library in South Carolina', she mentioned no African-Americans taking part in the work. And there was no mention of the Faith Cabin Libraries of Willie Lee Buffington.

Chapter 8 – Library building at full throttle in Georgia.

If anything bothered him concerning the exchange with Estellene Walker, Buffington brushed it aside and continued his work. Library building in Georgia was now full throttle. The Savannah *Morning News* chronicled the Halloween, 1948 dedication of the unit at Warren High School in Devereux, attended by several hundred people. The African-American farming community came together and built a concrete block structure, fit it with shelves and made hundreds of books available to the school and community.[159] That day, $1300 was raised to further the plan of teaching their children to read good books, and a bus was purchased so the children could ride to school. "We want our children educated and trained here at home," was their goal.[160]

Willie's heart was never far away from that sentiment of having children "educated and trained here at home." The course in Leadership that he taught at Paine was an exercise in practical education, as each member of the class fulfilled that calling at either the Bethlehem Community Center or the YMCA in Augusta. "Weekly meetings – just as the school year was over – were held with the school children in the five rural elementary schools in the community. Handicrafts, Scouting, 4H Club work and recreation constituted the program."[161] He trumped the educational system by some three decades in setting up after-school programs.

A second course, Rural Sociology, also enhanced this practical application, perhaps even more ardently. It afforded "almost a score of students to do some serious thinking about our rural population, their problems and significance to the national welfare," Buffington said. They participated on the community council, led worship services, offered programs on current events and wholesome recreation for youth, and researched problems facing owners of small family farms.[162] Practical good was always high on Willie's "to-do" list.

Buffington wrote to many of the women of the Southern Illinois Conference WSCS, who collected and sent the books, asking them to continue their efforts and send more volumes each year, especially by children's authors. Copies of the Savannah article were enclosed in his letters so they could share the victory of another "little lighthouse" being birthed.[163]

Always the innovator, Buffington utilized his photography skills in much of his work. At Devereux, he took more than 100 Kodachrome slides, intent on using them to make presentations and interest others in the work. In a letter to Mrs. Allen Newkirk, he was already exploring the possibility of visiting not only the Illinois Women's Conference, but also those in Indiana and Ohio to increase his list of donors.[164]

Two weeks later, November 13th, 1948, the Genesee (NY) Conference Unit was dedicated at Cartersville, with nearly 7000 books catalogued by library science students from Atlanta University. Much as with the Catherine Degen unit in Pendleton SC, the Cartersville Library held a special place in Buffington's heart. It served county citizens and eleven rural schools, but he was most pleased with the interracial cooperation ("no small achievement"). A white lawyer gave financial and moral support in helping black citizens secure the land; the Rotary Club of Georgia helped with funds for the building, and their president, Kendall Weisiger, announced at the dedication that the club would also give a shelf of biographies of such dignitaries as Booker T. Washington, George Washington Carver, and opera star Marian Anderson, among others. Robert L. Cousins, Director of Negro Schools for the Georgia Department of Education, stood proudly with the local citizens that day.[165] As at Devereux, Buffington continued the work with his camera and took scores of slides to include in future presentations.

He was also developing a strong yearning to pursue Faith Cabin Library work full time. His correspondence referenced more and more the workload of keeping up with the 50 odd libraries and teaching a full schedule at Paine College.

"I am ready to give my whole time to this important work...Your interest, prayers and support greatly encourages us in this task of interracial work in the South."[166] Again, he asked for "moral support and encouragement. Ask the good women to remember Faith Cabin Libraries when they pray."[167] And again, "We have been praying for many months, that some way would open up for us to give more time to this work."[168]

The North Indiana Unit at Swainsboro High and Industrial School, dedicated April 1st, 1949, was a work in progress. The women had sent books, eventually totaling 7000, two years before the two-room library opened. Buffington had taught an 8:00AM class at Paine, and then he "motored down" with his wife to be part of the festivities. She packed a sandwich lunch for them, since there was no extra money to buy a meal along the way. The school chorus sang several selections, all black and white ministers in the community were there, and a dozen white citizens who had helped with the project attended. In the thank-you letter he wrote for the Swainsboro residents to the women of the Conference, that strong commitment to library work was unmistakable.

"I have tried to quit several times since the work has been so hard—teaching a full schedule and trying to build ten or twelve libraries

74

a year---but I CANNOT QUIT. The needs and cries of the people served by this project would haunt me all my days."[169]

He hardly exaggerated the library expansion. In addition to the units at Devereux, Cartersville and Swainsboro, the growing Georgia list included: Dublin – Oconee High School (1947); Ashburn – Eureka High School (February, 1949); Jeffersonville – Jeffersonville Vocational Negro School (April, 1949); Baxley – Baxley Training School (May, 1949); Elberton – Blackwell High School (May, 1949); Douglas – Carver High School (May, 1949); Hartwell - Hartwell County Training School (August, 1949); and Eatonton – Eatonton and Butler-Booker High School (October, 1949). Jeffersonville principal W.E. West sent a letter of appreciation to Buffington, thanking him for the new library and letting him know he will be invited to the dedication as soon as it was scheduled. "We had enough books for most of the shelves," he said.[170] There was one last foray into South Carolina, as books were sent to St. Matthews and became part of the community library there.

Always, other duties needed his attention. A letter from W.D. Tolbert, principal of Bryan Street School in Conyers GA, required an answer on the procedure for securing books for a Faith Cabin Unit:

1. Provide housing for the library, and a teacher/librarian as staff.
2. Agree that the Faith Cabin Library serves both the school and community at large.
3. Pick up books in Augusta and transport to the library's location.[171]

Buffington also recommended to Tolbert that a trip to Lithonia and The Bruce Street School would prove worthwhile. Professor C.E. Flagg would enjoy showing him their efficiently run unit.

If anyone doubted the depth of the need, or the sincerity of those who so desperately sought to fill it, the letter from James R. Hightower would make them ardent believers. On behalf of Thomaston Training School and the Negro Committee on City Recreation in Thomaston GA, he asked Buffington to come at his earliest convenience "and plan with us for our Community Library.

"We have the room and the money necessary to install shelves," he continued. "We have about 6000 Negroes at Thomaston, and have no books for children or adults to read. We are sincerely trying to do something about our problem of recreation through reading."[172] The community secured its treasured center of learning.

From the glorious to the mundane, Buffington handled it all. In a letter to Mrs. L.T. Clark of the Southern Illinois Conference, he asked if the Wesleyan Service Guild might collect a love offering to help provide gas and oil for the Jeep Station Wagon. His plan, he told her, was to visit all 50 operating libraries during the spring of 1949.[173] That killer schedule never let up for him.

Perhaps it was that very schedule, which put most working men to shame, that led to the quandary. He enjoyed teaching; yet, it was the library work that stirred his blood. Giving everything he had to both, and being a husband and father, made him far older than his 40 years. Buffington confided not just in some Faith Cabin benefactors, but to individuals who had the resources to create a way for him to enter the library work full time. There was so much left to do, and he sensed that there would never be enough time to reach all those who needed his help.

Earl Brown, executive secretary for the Methodist Church Board of Missions, was at work in late 1948 "on a projection that I think will continue the service under your leadership." Half of the salary would come from the Board, and the other half from the Methodist Women's Division.[174] Buffington answered the letter the same day it arrived, and eight days later was informed by Brown that he would take the recommendation to the Executive Committee.[175]

Work took a toll on his family as well. Daughter Ethel Margaret remembered threats against her father by local Ku Klux Klan chapters, and she feared being singled out because of his livelihood. Buffington tried to protect his children by enrolling them in school districts away from his work, but to little avail. Though her fears were not realized at the hands of Klan members, she was ridiculed by her classmates because of her father's reputation for helping African-Americans.[176] She also remembered her brother having more problems than she did, so much so that Willie Jr. spent his high school years (1947 – 1949) in Rome GA, graduating from his father's alma mater, the Martha Berry School. There was a host of letters from father to son, about studying hard, keeping up his grades, and registering for the draft deferment while still in school. Family, teaching, and building libraries were worlds in collision as the 1950's came on the horizon.

The new decade opened with an inspiring letter regarding the library in Quitman GA. Louise Bennett, secretary of the Brooks County Chamber of Commerce, first apologized for being behind schedule in the construction phase, noting "you may know something about government delays!" But now the books were on the shelves, and local citizens added to their numbers. "I am quite sure that this library will be one of the greatest assets in our work with the young and old Negro citizens that we can ever have."[177]

With such encouragement, Buffington accelerated his own efforts to find the adequate funding source that would allow him to build his libraries full-time, and he moved from the Methodist Church Board of Missions to the Home Missions Council of North America. Their letterhead described the group as "The Interchurch Agency of Home Mission Boards and Societies of Twenty Three Denominations." It was a simple matter of numbers that led him to seek this broader base of support.

Buffington sent a long letter to Dr. George Nace, executive secretary of the HMC, on April 29, 1950, enclosing published articles about the Faith Cabin mission. Books, he noted, were given by friends "of all denominations and none," and when a community could provide a building and staff, a portion of the books was immediately re-directed to that location. "The cooperation between the races elicited in these efforts is worthwhile in addition to providing the Negro people with a library facility." Pleasantries were afforded little time and space. He even offered to travel to New York City to speak with Nace, though no funds were available.

"With 61 libraries, we should have, full time, some secretarial help and some aid for travel. This project has always enjoyed a wide appeal, and it seems wise to appeal to your organization for help, rather than limiting financial help to one denomination." Or to one institution, he might have added.

Some paragraphs bared raw nerves about his position at Paine College. "Overwork...trying to keep abreast of 61 libraries...and a teaching position where one is responsible for the growth of students...saps energy, prevents me from having the satisfaction that a thorough job is being done in either area...and does not seem to be good common sense or good religion. I could never be happy in the knowledge that I gave up Faith Cabin Libraries and retained a job that paid a salary. Yet, I must have income for the family."

It was one of the few times Buffington mentioned money, or the sacrifices his family made to ensure that his mission of providing for his African-American friends continued. After the February 11th, 1949 dedication at Ashburn GA, he was told by the college that there could be no more travel, even though library openings would soon occur at Swainsboro (April 1st), Jeffersonville (April 21st), Baxley (May 1st), Elberton (May 22nd), and Douglas (May 22nd). He remonstrated, "SO FAR AS THE ADMINISTRATION OF THE COLLEGE WAS CONCERNED NO ONE FROM PAINE COLLEGE SHOULD BE AT

THE DEDICATIONS even when it is maintained that this work should be done through the college."

The letter closed with eight questions posed to Nace, and spoke to the faulty logic of having Paine continue as sponsor of the work. "What gives Paine College the right to take over – without consultation a work nurtured and developed by a staff member before he joined the staff...Seems like strange ethics creeping in somewhere!" Stressing that he was seldom consulted about the direction of the Faith Cabin Library work, he made his final stand and asked, "IS IT A WISE POLICY TO MAKE THIS PROJECT WHICH HAS BEEN SUPPORTED THROUGH THE YEARS BY PEOPLE OF MANY DENOMINATIONS and would have never come into being with just Methodist support (as admirable as that has been since 1947)? Doesn't such a move limit the scope of its support in terms of books?"[178]

As thorough and lengthy as this letter to Nace is, it represented just the beginning of Buffington's quest for a wider base of support for Faith Cabin Libraries. Don F. Pielstick, Associate Secretary of the Home Missions Council, answered Buffington and informed him that the Executive Secretary "seeks wider consideration of your program before we make any definite reply" and referred it to the entire Southeastern Inter-Council Office. If "hearty approval" was forthcoming, Pielstick continued, then they would bring the Faith Cabin Library financing before the Administrative Committee for consideration. "This seems to be about as much as we can do at present." Pielstick noted that he has heard of Buffington's libraries many times, and has felt favorable toward them.[179]

If the letter to Nace was the earthquake, then the ten-letter barrage of May 11th and 12th constituted a formidable series of powerful aftershocks. Nine of those letters were sent on the 11th as Buffington marshaled all his forces. W.F. Quillian, president of Wesleyan College, Macon GA, who supplied Buffington with the list of Southeastern Inter-Council board members, heard the passionate message that was to be repeated again and again. "The work is needed...but I cannot continue with such a heavy physical load in teaching and carrying responsibilities for this work. With 61 communities, whither with or now building a library – in which we have given grant-in-aid books – that alone would be a full-time job just supervising and keeping replenished with books...but we shall be building more."[180]

The appeal to Dr. Edward G. Mackey, Home Missions Council, spoke to the very reason Faith Cabin Libraries existed. "Anything you can do to help secure adequate support to enable me to donate full time to this work will be advancing the cause of Christian education among our Negro people across the state. I am anxious that the work be carried on in the name of the Christian Church."[181]

Often Buffington asked the recipients of these letters to rally the troops. Bishop Arthur Moore was asked to speak with board member Dr. Forrest Weir. Robert Cousins, Georgia Director of Negro Education, received a list of members of the Southeastern Inter-Council Office Board, and was asked to contact those living in the Atlanta area who might help the cause. To Nelle Morton, general secretary of the Fellowship of Christian Churchwomen (who organized interracial youth camps and conferences), he confessed that "if the project is to continue, it demands the full time of a director" and asked for her support. Rev. A.L. Gilmore was told, "You will be helping us to serve thousands of our Negro people with reading facilities in the name of the Church of Christ" (the Savior, not the denomination), and was given the names of Mrs. B.E. Mays (wife of the Morehouse College president) and others as references. Mrs. David Jones of Bennett College would serve a most noble effort with her support. "You will be helping to bring library facilities to thousands of our people sadly in need of such facilities."

Three other members, like Quillian, happened to be chief executive officers at institutions of higher learning. To Dr. J.M. Ellison (Virginia Union University), Buffington shared his fear that the Inter-Council board might not have sufficient knowledge of the Faith Cabin Library work, and asked for his strong voice of support. Much the same message went to Dr. F. D. Patterson (Tuskegee Institute), noting that 30 libraries had been founded in rural communities these past six years, and that "their work has been done on the 'second mile' (unpaid hours)". The appeal to Dr. Harry Richardson (Gammon Theological Seminary, Atlanta) was more complex because President Peters of Paine College and Richardson had previously discussed Gammon taking the Faith Cabin sponsorship. Buffington expressed his belief that the college assuming that role gained tremendous public relations value.

The flurry of correspondence came full circle with a second letter from Louise Bennett, secretary of the Brooks County Chamber of Commerce, extolling the project in Quitman GA. She enclosed a copy of a letter written to Dr. Forrest Weir about Buffington. "It is growing too large for one person to handle, (and) you have given so generously of your own time and money and efforts. I cannot think of a much more valuable Home Mission movement than that of adequate education through the right type of books."[182]

Southeastern Inter-Council Board members urged Buffington to be present at their May 25th Advisory Council meeting to answer questions on behalf of the Faith Cabin Libraries. That was impossible,

Willie replied, because his attendance was required at the Paine College Board of Trustee meeting that same day, to report on the status of the program. His report would go into far greater detail than perhaps any trustee really wanted to hear.

Chapter 9 – "The first and primary aim is people and libraries."

That May 25th meeting of the Paine College Board of Trustees featured Buffington's report on Faith Cabin Library work during the past year, an impressive list of accomplishments. He moved to the podium in front of the room and his gaze swept across the faces of distinguished men and women in attendance. Edwin Maynard's article in *Kiwanis Magazine*, he reminded them, had just appeared in February, and was proof of that "positive PR" ever present in the work. The author certainly was no stranger to the college or to Buffington – he learned of both while on an earlier assignment for the *Christian Advocate* for a series of articles on the progress of race relations.[183]

There were three library dedications of particular interest to the Board. In Eatonton GA (October, 1949) "the Negro school is a disgrace to American democracy", but educational and religious leadership offered hope for a brighter future. The Quitman GA unit at Brooks County High School (May 15, 1950) came about through a spirit of black and white cooperation that was particularly striking. That spirit was conspicuous by its absence in Donaldsonville GA (May 15, 1950). Though started more than two years earlier, progress lagged due to Ku Klux Klan activity. A Klan committee censored books in black *and* white libraries, and no controversial items on race (certainly nothing approaching the idea of equality) were allowed.[184] It was not surprising, then, that Bishop Arthur Mozee, trustee president, noted that "READING ABILITY (in high school) is of such a low level that it is well nigh impossible for many of the students (at Paine) to do college work."[185]

Buffington continued. Nearly 6000 books were shipped to Sylvania GA to replace the losses when the Screven County Negro School burned two months earlier. Plans moved forward to construct a new unit in Homerville, and Buffington had travelled there to speak with local black citizens, Methodist women and educational leaders. He was touched by the gift of one illiterate black laborer, who donated 500 concrete blocks to start the foundation of the new building.[186] His old friend, Dr. Channing Tobias, accompanied him on a visit to the library at Sandersville GA in February 1950, and the two continued on to Milledgeville to discuss planting a new unit there.

Buffington's opening remarks concluded with a careful summation of his travels on behalf of the college during the preceding year, and it was a list to inspire fatigue. He participated in a School of Missions in both the New Jersey and New York East conferences in

July, 1949, repaying their many kindnesses in donating books. He addressed the annual meeting of the Ohio WSCS later that summer, and attended both the anniversary celebration of the Cartersville GA library and the Georgia Negro Principal's Conference in Albany GA in November, 1949. That same month there were community meetings in Saluda SC and in Haddock GA, where there was a growing interest in improving race relations. He found time to represent Paine at three Methodist Church meetings: the North Carolina Annual Conference in November, 1949; and both the Macon GA and Savannah GA District conferences in January, 1950.[187]

Then he stopped, took a deep breath, and asked, "Is the administration of Paine College interested in doing a real job out in the rural communities where Faith Cabin Libraries are located?" Buffington stated what he so often heard about the work, namely "it's dramatic, it has public appeal". What he had come to believe, though, was that only the "dramatic", the "appeal", and the "money raising angle" aroused any interest. He continued:

"...but THE FIRST AND PRIMARY AIM IS PEOPLE AND LIBRARIES. The social and economic situation of so many Negro people coupled with inequalities in education is a major social problem, and it would be a sin in the sight of God and man to exploit these conditions and the human suffering in rural areas for 'dramatic effect' and 'money raising appeal'. I cannot knowingly become a party to such procedure."[188] The silence that followed seemed much, much longer than a few ticks from the clock. Some of those seated met his gaze. Most did not.

He broke the tension in a most practical manner, talking dollars and cents. Paine's appropriation to his work, $100 per month, was handled on an item-by-item basis, and Buffington only asked that the amount be deposited for use "without permission for every 3 cent stamp". He also talked about the mileage on the Faith Cabin Library's Jeep station wagon, a more complicated issue since it needed replacing. Noting that it was used for college publicity, he asked either for a $25 government bond or for $25 to be set aside in an account so the purchase of a new vehicle could eventually be made. He explained that "it warns me against depending upon Paine College for transportation for this work."[189]

Though these distinguished people were hearing things they would rather have not, none denied the passion and singular vision of this man whose work benefited so many of the families and communities represented in the college's own student body. More positive public relations were not far behind, this time as Henry Sprinkle's "The Miracle of Books" appeared in the September issue of *World Outlook*:

"In scores of instances the entire neighborhood, black and white, has been enriched by the experience of voluntary interracial cooperation in the battle against ignorance, illiteracy, and inadequate opportunity for the underprivileged."[190] It was such a good ministry, the directors knew that. Why did the director have to be so petulant?

Buffington was nothing if not a man of action. Deeply anchored in his faith and the work that sprang from it, he understood that sometimes God required him to do the heavy lifting. This was one of those times and he plowed ahead in those days after the meeting. First, in a memo to Dr. Edgar Love (a Bishop for the black congregations in the segregated Methodist Church), he said, "The work is the important thing because it serves a people in need of help."[191]

He saw three immediate advantages to the sponsorship by the Home Missions Council: (1) he would be able to give full time to Faith Cabin Libraries; (2) more resources could be tapped, since they were supported by 13 leading Protestant denominations; and (3) interracial contacts would be broadened, with an expanded integration of the library work with educational and religious organizations in a communities.[192]

Nace, the Home Mission Council's executive secretary, followed through as well, referring the sponsorship request directly to the Southeastern Inter-Office Board, where a committee formed, studied and submitted its findings to Don Pielstick. Dr. E.C. Peters, Paine's president and Buffington's advocate, also supported the new arrangement, though there must have been a measure of heartache after so many years spent with the man and his mission.

Pielstick's letter arrived in Augusta in early November, and among other things asked for a listing of the library locations. Buffington obliged, and the return correspondence included descriptions of his field work, always ongoing, and always close to his heart.

"I was with the Methodist Youth Fellowship this past Sunday night in that community (Saluda) talking about our responsibilities for our Negro neighbors. This attempt at bettering race relations at the grass roots level appeals to me. More reality in our day-to-day practice of our great Christian religion is one of the crying needs of this critical hour."[193]

The sponsorship resolution was on the table for everyone to talk about, but a quick answer was not forthcoming. Libraries, though, were being built, requests for more continued to come in, and people's lives were being changed. Willie sensed that the critical hour was upon him, and it extended far beyond cabins and books.

Students knew that the libraries were a solid recruiting tool for the college, and many of them helped sort the books by subject matter. Cataloging, though, was left for library of science majors. Astute observers, such as Paine College student Maurice Cherry, looked past the library movement and saw the man whose work toward interracial understanding was central in the coming crest of the civil rights movement.

"I can still hear him saying to us in class, '*We* will have to fight so *we* can be free.' He always associated himself with us, and we admired that. Students saw Buffington as a person rather than a white man, a man for the season who brought hope to many wearied by long years of striving. He never wanted attention for himself.

"He saw a great need and met it head on," Dr. Cherry recalled. "We respectfully called him 'Dr. Buffington', even though he wasn't a PhD, and we affectionately called him 'Buff' out of earshot, because he meant so much to us."[194]

"And this is how I made my payment to mankind…"

The line was from a radio program that represented Faith Cabin Library's ongoing presence on the national stage. *Cavalcade of America*, sponsored by the DuPont Company, created the drama "Uncle Eury's Dollar" from a well-conceived formula of documenting historical events using stories of individual courage, triumph of the human spirit against all odds, and humanitarian progress. If anyone had questions about the public relations impact of the libraries, *Cavalcade* offered emphatic answers.

There were the usual glitches that arose during such creative ventures. "We want to assure you that the actor impersonating you will not use the extreme Southern accent to which you object." Gwendolyn Owen, employed by the company that prepared the program for DuPont, worked closely with Buffington to make certain the final draft measured up to the real story. It was a rewarding effort for all involved.

"I greatly enjoyed talking with you on the phone," she said, "and we are all most grateful to you for the help and cooperation you have given us."[195]

"Uncle Eury's Dollar", airing on March 31, 1951, brought to life the friendship of Buffington and Euriah Simpkins, and detailed what they accomplished together to make improved race relations more than just a dream. The drama, born from a one page picture article in *American Magazine* (October, 1950), drew more than lightweights to the project. Writer Morton Wishengrad fashioned the touching story, much as he would do six years later with *Rope Dancers*, a 1958 Tony Award nominee. Robert Cummings portrayed Buffington and was but three years away from a memorable role in Alfred Hitchcock's *Dial M For Murder*. Juano Hernandez stirred the audience as Euriah Simpkins, much as he did as Lucas Beauchamp in William Faulkner's *Intruder In The Dust*, for which he had received a 1949 Tony Award nomination.

As *Cavalcade of America* moved from radio to television in 1952, "Uncle Eury's Dollar" was one of the episodes that made the transition to the small screen. "But the words of Professor Eury Simpkins...they were words I didn't forget," said Cummings/Buffington. And neither did a lot of other people. The show drew the largest influx of fan mail from any company production, more than 800 letters making their way from New York City to Augusta, asking for ways to help the cause. Even the star of the show became an admirer.

Cummings wrote, "My own part was not a difficult one as the story itself created such a wonderfully sympathetic feeling in anyone listening, how this simple but impressive man started and devoted himself to this wonderful cause."[196]

"When *Cavalcade of America* aired "Uncle Eury's Dollar", everyone sat around the radio in the library and listened," Dr. Maurice Cherry recalled with a special fondness." [197]

But a special post arrived earlier than the others, not from some distant locale, and it meant the world to Buffington. Dr. B.E. Geer, the Furman College president who made it possible for the young man to earn a degree, and who supported his efforts toward interracial cooperation, wrote the day after the program aired.

"I should like to hear from you at your leisure and to know something of your present work...You are *doing* sociology, not merely telling about it in a classroom."[198]

Geer always held Willie Lee in high esteem. The accomplishments, the work ethic and the big heart told him everything he needed to know. Dr. Cherry could not have agreed more with Dr. Geer's assertion. A transfer student to Paine in 1949, Cherry took every course in sociology taught by Buffington, except for one that could not be worked into his schedule. Theirs was a special relationship, and he noted that most of his classmates were equally impressed.

"Most students were from families who sacrificed to send their children to college, but none of us had come from such lowly circumstances as Dr. Buffington.[199] With his southern drawl, we were tempted not to take his lecture/discussion approach in the classroom very seriously.

"We thought it wasn't necessary, and felt we would have an easy ride in that particular course. I thought that way once, until he returned a test and my grade was *very* low. I learned that behind that drawl he was all business, and was certainly *not* paternalistic. I did not make that mistake again."[200]

When different versions of the *Bible* were published and copies sent to the college, Buffington always steered one in Cherry's direction. He did the same with new editions of *Gospel Parallels*. "He shared so much of himself with us, his knowledge and experiences, that when I went to seminary I was not overwhelmed."[201]

Dr. Cherry, who graduated in 1952 and returned to Paine as college chaplain in 1959, remembered times his friend could get a bit wrapped up in the subject matter. Buffington often preached at vespers on Sunday evenings, an event with mandatory attendance. "You told us stuff we didn't need to know!", many of the students would good naturedly chide him. It was their way of commenting on a particularly long-winded delivery.[202] Buffington took it all in stride, though there was no report on whether subsequent talks were shorter.

The determination in that heart was no more evident than on March 16th, the day Buffington notified Dr. E.C. Peters that he would be unavailable to teach sociology at Paine College the next academic year. Faith Cabin Libraries would no longer play second fiddle to college duties.[203]

Willie remembered the acrimonious confrontation at the previous year's meeting, and knew that his decision not to teach would add fuel to the fire during the upcoming gathering. So be it. He battled unfavorable odds all his life, and one more skirmish was not going to derail his work. But there was a whisper from deep inside. Words that had flown across air waves a few days before when "Uncle Eury's Dollar" was broadcast, were now meant only for him.

"Will you spend your life nursing a grudge against your brother?"

He remembered the warm summer day long ago in the backwoods outside Saluda. The broken mudpies. His devil of a little brother laughing and running off. His own tears. The hate he felt. Euriah Simpkins reminded him then that hating his brother was wrong, and reminded him again today that his was a journey of reconciliation anchored in the work called the Faith Cabin Libraries. He folded Geer's letter and placed it in a desk drawer.

"Clara!" He called to his wife, his hand on the back doorknob. "I'm out for a walk. A few things I've got to sort out. I need…"

"We'll talk when you get back. I'm sure there will be a lot to discuss."

As he cut across the yard and made the sidewalk on Central Avenue, he said quietly, "There's got to be a different tone at this year's meeting."

Buffington's opening address on May 24th, 1951 to the Board of Trustees (the Faith Cabin Library Board was also present) was just that as he posed the question, "What is the relationship of Paine College to Faith Cabin Libraries?" After a pause, he began answering.

"There has been a very serious misunderstanding along the way, and for the sake of those who benefit from this service, I welcome the meeting of this committee to help clarify a situation that has caused me untold anxiety and heartache...may all your deliberations be in accordance with the spirit and purpose of Christ..."[204]

He was conciliatory, yet maintained a pragmatic view of a burgeoning workload tempered with self-deprecating humor. "I have attempted to do my best with every assignment, even at personal sacrifice of time, energy and a meager salary...lately I have been told that I am developing into a 'chronic whiner' (alas, I thought it was a 'martyr complex'). From 1935 to 1942 we, a family of four, lived on less than $500 per year, while I was pursuing educational advantages, and we didn't exploit friends of Faith Cabin Library for funds, and we didn't grumble..."[205]

Sixty three (63) libraries now demanded his attention, with enough books arriving to create 10 new ones each year, and Buffington's vision was for continued expansion, either under the auspices of the college, the Methodist Church, or another Christian agency. That year alone, between 25,000 and 30,000 books were received and processed by him, his wife, and one student helper. He and Clara handled all the correspondence that acknowledged the many sources of donations and directed the books to recipient communities. He even arranged photograph displays of the work, highlighting gifts from the Detroit and Port Huron (Michigan) districts, the Episcopal Church Periodical Club (Washington State), and the Delta Kappa Gamma Society of Ottawa Illinois.[206] He also shared the disappointments, including a folder provided to churches during Race Relations Day asking for an offering for "further development of the work of Faith Cabin Libraries." No money came from the appeal.[207]

Unlike the year before, when Buffington stood his ground alone, the Faith Cabin Library Board of Directors forwarded nine recommendations to the trustees. Six referred primarily to routine duties and reporting structures: that the college, for instance, remained the disbursing agent for all appropriations to the libraries; and the work space for book disbursements be made available at no cost. Three were much more significant, and spelled out in detail by chairwoman Mrs. Sadie Mays: that Buffington be released from teaching and other regular duties at Paine; that the Division of Home Missions and Church Extension pay the rent for his home on Central Avenue directly to the college; and that all special funds coming to Buffington as director of the Faith Cabin Libraries be turned over to the college for proper recording and disbursement. Compromise was the order of the day.

Mrs. Mayes, wife of Benjamin Mays, president of Morehouse College, finished her presentation by reminding the trustees that this significant movement grew from Buffington's deep concern for the welfare of African Americans living in rural areas, and used the library at Ashburn GA for her example. Turner County had 22 rural schools for black children, nearly half meeting in churches; there was but one high school with three buildings, and two of those were in bad repair. Into this need he stepped, and together with local leaders saw that lumber was provided. Parents raised money for the siding, women from the white Methodist churches gave 24 chairs, and books came from the Newark NJ Conference of the Women's Society of Christian Services.[208]

She gave Willie a smile as she returned to her seat, the day growing a bit brighter for all concerned, as a well devised and acceptable plan was finally on the table.

He wrote to her within the week, pledging "to the Committee my best spirit, my best efforts and wholehearted cooperation…and this applies to the administration of Paine College, too. We shall pray and work that Faith Cabin Libraries will make an effective contribution to Christian education and human relations, and bring only credit to the illustrious record of Paine College and the missionary outreach of the Methodist Church."[209]

The libraries never ceased to be a source of inspiration to people, whether patron or donor, as that magical "PR" shone brightly. Mrs. W.A. Payton, in her 80's, gave 16,465 pounds of books to the cause, and she pre-paid the freight for 107 boxes shipped from Danville IL. The naming of the library at Elberton GA, the Illinois Conference Unit, was done primarily in her honor.[210]Sorting the books on those shelves late one evening, Willie thought he heard Mr. Simpkins' voice carried on the September breeze, and he could only smile at the continued fulfillment of his friend's prophetic utterance years before: "God will provide."

"He always does," Willie said aloud. The folks working alongside hardly noticed.

Cataloging and sorting.
Courtesy Caroliniana Library.

Chapter 10 – Mr. Buffington, full-time director.

Beginning with the 1951-52 academic year, there were new sources of income for the director's position. The Division of Missions-Board of Missions of the Methodist Church, and the Women's Division of Christian Service of the Methodist Church, paid his salary *plus* $100 per month for travel expenses.[211] Buffington gave out the information, but also continued to stress his connection with Paine.

"...with the help of two agencies of the Board of Missions of the Methodist Church, the college released me for full-time work in this project (Faith Cabin Libraries). I do, however, teach the course in Marriage and the Family in the fall semester, and Rural Community Life in the spring semester to keep my contact with the student generation."[212]

He wasted little time putting that travel stipend to good use, and in July visited the South Carolina libraries of Belton, Fountain Inn, Owings, Gray Court, Chapman's Grove, Pendleton and Easley. The Belton visit was especially meaningful, as Buffington renewed the acquaintance of Cooledge Johnson, a former Benedict College student, now school principal there.[213]There was promise of more "roadwork" to come, and the mileage on the old Jeep wagon, which had averaged nearly 15000 miles a year since 1947, would certainly increase "now that relief had been provided from classroom duties."[214]

All but eight libraries received a visit from May 1951 through May 1952 as Buffington counseled with school and library personnel. These visits usually doubled as book deliveries. He was forever the Paine booster, calling on high school principals and graduating classes, administering tests to determine scholarship awards and sharing his conviction about "the importance of Paine College in the total kingdom program of the Church" at Methodist district conferences.[215]

1952: Ralph Ellison's novel, *Invisible Man*, wins the National Book Award.

Buffington added another five new units to the growing network of libraries now spreading across the Peach State. When the Jesup facility was dedicated on May 13, 1952, the ceremony was broadcast over the local radio station. With a bit less fanfare, though no less important, libraries at Hephzibah, Crawfordville, Lumber City, Milledgeville, and Lawrenceville began to offer their treasures to communities longing for books. And the ladies of Wellesley College (MA) collected volumes for an as yet undetermined site.[216] The old

90

station wagon also benefited from Faith Cabin Library friends, as donations paid for major repairs, with $456.40 left to begin the new fiscal year. Thankfully, the FCL Board of Directors also budgeted $2000 to replace the aging Jeep, which had now amassed 90,000 hard miles of service.[217]

Two articles written by his old friend and Paine colleague, Emma C.W. Gray, appeared in the Fall Quarter *Church School Literature*. At the suggestion of Reverend Ray Murray, Adult Publications editor at David Cook Publishing Company, all books donated by readers of Ms. Gray would create a memorial collection in honor of Euriah Simpkins.[218] Buffington's photography talents also brought benefits, and in a most unusual fashion. A set of 2 x 2 Kodachrome slides was loaned to a particular Vacation Bible School, where leaders suggested that a movie be made of Faith Cabin Library work. They were serious enough to give the camera, while another donation provided the film. Plans were made for two movies: one of Paine College and its campus programs, and a second of the libraries in use.[219] The movies were indeed made, and are now part of the Caroliniana Collection, University of South Carolina, Columbia SC.

Even with all of this, Buffington talked of the joy of leading chapel at Paine College during Holy Week, and how much he missed the daily classroom contact with students. It was something that, for all of his protests, he could never wholly give up, and a generation of those college kids was forever grateful. He managed to fit it all into a 24 hour day.

There was always one certainty where the good professor was concerned: it was full speed ahead with the coming of a new year. Three new libraries were christened: Woodbine, Camden County (GA), Ralph Bunche High School; Ocilla, Irwin County (GA), Ocilla Negro and Industrial High School; and Ludowici, Long County (GA) Walker High School. With books given by Ms. Gray's readers and by the Women's Auxiliary of Trinity Episcopal Church, Williamsport PA, these were added to the 67 beacons of light already shining. "Each new library will continue towards the enrichment of school and community life," Buffington said.[220] He also gave ongoing attention to improving existing locations, and continued to combine student recruitment with each visit.

Alas, faithful sidekick and dependable transportation, the 1947 Jeep was traded in (at 120,000 miles) on a 1953 model equipped with "helping springs" that promised a better ride when loaded down with books.[221] Individual donors came through so there was no payment hardship or borrowing. Old '47 had given its very best.

Four other items, in addition to Gray's "A Man and His Ministry of Books" (which inspired 10,000 volumes donated to the Ocilla unit), made their way into print and into the hearts of people across the country. "Share a Book, Sister" was published in *Methodist Woman* in October of 1952; the pamphlet *A Dime's Worth of Books* came from the presses of the University of Virginia; a chapter for *The Wonderful World of Books* (New American Library) was contributed by Buffington the same year; and an article for Norman Vincent Peale's *Guideposts Magazine* ran in March, 1953. This last piece generated interest from the young people of Dunlee Presbyterian Church, Omaha NE; they collected 1200 books, which were used to replace the library in Edgefield SC, lost in a fire.[222]

August 13th, 1953: President Dwight D. Eisenhower signs Executive Order 10479, establishing the anti-discrimination Committee on Government Contracts.

1953: James Baldwin's autobiography *Go Tell It On The Mountain* is published.

It was the actions of individuals toward their less fortunate brothers and sisters, like the kids from Nebraska, which touched Willie Lee deeply. The Monmouth NJ County Organization for Social Services held an auction, cleared $200, and promptly sent a magazine subscription to one of the libraries.[223] Thousands of such kindnesses graced mail routes from across the county to the small Augusta college.

May 17th, 1954. The United States Supreme Court, in Brown vs. Board of Education of Topeka KS, rules that segregation in public schools is unconstitutional. Separate educational facilities, the justices note, are inherently unequal.

Several supporters suggested that *Brown vs. Board of Education*, concerning public schools in seventeen states and the District of Columbia, rendered the services of the libraries unnecessary. Buffington believed otherwise. "Until the changes are made," he said, "the need for books given by Faith Cabin Libraries remains, as does the need for the spirit of goodwill in which the attempt was made."[224]

"So now everyone is telling you the battle is over when the wind picked up in the west and blew a gust of common sense across the plains and toward us southern folks. Nothing ever comes that easy, boy. So…"

Winter gusts blew rain through the glow of streetlights, and Willie thought he saw the drops beginning to turn to ice. "So, what are you going to do?"

One set of footfalls clicked on the wet pavement. Willie gladly carried on the conversation.

"What we've done all along, sir. Put books in the hands of those who never had them. Put an education within their grasp. Help them make their way. Help them make a better life. Be in the line of fire with them, because things will get worse before they get better."

He imagined the strong hand on his shoulder, and felt the wind pick up and carry Euriah's words across time. "God will provide, son."

"Yes, sir," Willie said aloud as he walked past the library on campus. "Preparation meeting opportunity." The security guard at his station waved, not at all surprised to see "Buff" out walking in the hours just after midnight.

January 5th, 1955: Marian Anderson becomes the first African-American to perform with the New York Metropolitan Opera.

August 28th, 1955: Emmett Till, a black teen from Chicago, is abducted from his uncle's home in Money, MS by two white men after supposedly whistling at a white woman. His body is found three days later.

December 1st, 1955. Rosa Parks is arrested in Montgomery AL for refusing to give her seat to a white passenger and move to the back of the bus.

Having a late start getting his education, Willie Lee never missed an opportunity to enhance his intellectual skills.

"It is a pleasure to notify you," wrote A.K. Kirby, an associate dean at the University of North Carolina at Chapel Hill, "that you have been admitted to the Graduate School for the purpose of undertaking a program in the Department of Sociology and Anthropology beginning in the first Summer Session which opens on June 7th, 1956."[225]Specifically, he studied Marriage and Family Living with Dr. Reuben Hill, and Rural Community Relationships with Dr. Samuel Hobbs Jr.[226]

Buffington thanked members of the Southern Fellowship Fund for providing the grant-in-aid that made his continuing education possible. His expression of gratitude did not preclude his request of another for the next summer. "...I would like to plan to visit, and confer with leaders and youth, in as many of the State and Regional church conferences…both white and Negro, in the Southeast." [227]Eyes on the goal left little time for subtlety or shyness.

November 5th, 1956: The first episode of the *Nat King Cole Show* airs on national television, and has a run of 13 months.

Where Buffington was concerned, there were two constants: more books for libraries; and more requests for building them. The Thomason GA unit received 700 books from the 5th grade of the Friends School in Baltimore MD (their third time donating), and they matched that total for the elementary school in Johnston SC.[228] In short order, Margaret Walker presented a workshop for Faith Cabin Libraries in the Roberta GA library (October 17th, 1956); the Franklin GA library was dedicated as part of the observance of National Book Week (November 29th, 1956); and 4000 new books were received from Spencer Press of Chicago (January, 1957), with freight paid by the Sears & Roebuck Foundation. Most heartwarming was the 2300 pounds of books sent by Mrs. W.A. Payton, which filled the library of Blackwell Memorial School in Elberton GA. An elderly widow and member of St. James Methodist Church in Danville IL, and weighing but 100 pounds herself, she sorted and packed the books, and arranged for shipment.[229]

January – February, 1957: Martin Luther King Jr., Charles Steele and Fred Shuttleworth establish the Southern Leadership Conference, with King as its first president. The organization is a major force in galvanizing the civil rights movement based on non-violence and civil disobedience.

September 25th, 1957. President Dwight D. Eisenhower sends federal National Guard troops to assure that nine African American students are able to enroll at Central High School in Little Rock, AR.

From Cairo, Jackson County and Winder City GA came heartfelt requests for books to benefit their young people. Erma Cameron (librarian) and Daniel Grant (principal) from Cairo and the Washington Consolidated School, wrote that "it will mean so much to us if we could get help from you, because our school will not be accredited until our library has been brought up-to-date. The library is deficient in books."[230]

Robert Cousins, the Georgia Director of Negro Education, was a great ally and supporter of Buffington's. He encouraged Frary Elrod,

Superintendent of the Jackson County School System,[231] and D.F. Osborne, Superintendent of the Winder City School System,[232] to contact Buffington, invite him to the schools, and request 1500 volumes each to fill their libraries. Willie Lee added these locations to the Faith Cabin Library fold.

In the midst of celebrating Paine College's 75th anniversary and Faith Cabin's 25th, the ever vigilant founder was at his post, worrying about finances. "We are faced with a curtailment of travel unless we can secure a small increase in expense funds...we shall likely have a four cent stamp...gas is up two cents a gallon; and it is almost impossible to get a motel room for less than $4.00 per night."[233]

For all the years Buffington collected books for his precious libraries, it seemed there was always a shortage of children's books. And certainly, for all the writers and journalists who chronicled the Faith Cabin movement, there was no one who wrote children's literature. To some degree, both needs were delightfully filled in February, 1958, when Seth Harmon's "A Book for Benjy" was published in *Trails for Juniors*. It was called semi-fictional, and was illustrated with a drawing of the bulletin board at the Franklin GA library.[234]

January 15th, 1958: Willie O'Ree breaks the color barrier in the National Hockey League as he plays his first game for the Boston Bruins.

1958: Paul Robeson's autobiography, *Here I Stand*, is published.

Herman Styler was another writer who never forgot the difference Buffington made in these times, both with his libraries and his efforts toward making interracial understanding a reality in his native South. Author of "He Worked Wonders – with Faith and a Dime!" (*Coronet Magazine*, June, 1947), he nominated Willie for the 10th annual Lane Bryant Award for 1957 (presented in November of 1958). For a humble man whose life's work was summed up in that one word motto adorning the libraries – "Others" – he was uncomfortable with such fanfare. Yet, the work, placed on a national stage, would do so much good.

This distinguished award was established "to inspire and encourage the volunteer efforts that benefit the American home and community", and Buffington was chosen for the individual award (there was also a group recognition). The award, and its $1000 stipend, sought out those who served rather than those who were much honored, and whose courage placed them on the front lines in the battles for human liberties. The judges over the years read like a Who's Who of American life: CBS president Frank Stanton; Congresswoman Frances Bolton; Dr. George Gallup; Senator John Kennedy; Dr. Margaret Mead; Pearl Buck; Senator Hubert Humphrey; and J.C. Penney.[235]

The ceremony was covered locally and nationally. Both the Augusta GA *Herald* (November 13th, 1958) and *Chronicle* (November 14th), ran stories, as did *Jet Magazine* (November 27th). It was in the hometown *Herald* that a Buffington quote underscored the changes would define the coming decade. "This (access to books) is very important to the complete development of persons who can successfully take their places in our complex social order."[236] But before he faced the 1960's, there were losses that wounded him nearly as deeply as did the death of Euriah Simpkins years before.

January 12th, 1959: Motown Records is founded by Berry Gordy.

1959: Lorraine Hansberry's *A Raisin In The Sun* makes its Broadway debut. The 1961 film will star Sidney Portier.

In 1959, both Emma C.W. Gray and Dr. E.C. Peters passed away. Gray, the Dean of Women at Paine, was always an ardent supporter of Faith Cabin work, and wrote articles that highlighted Buffington's work through the years. President Peters was there from the beginning. His wife attended the dedication of the very first Faith Cabin Library, the Annie Bodie Unit, at Plum Branch. He was there when Willie Lee graduated from high school, and later fulfilled his promise to bring the young man to Paine College as a teacher. And he wrote articles in support of the library movement. Though the two men had their differences of opinion on the handling of Faith Cabin Libraries by the college, after the passing of years Buffington could admit to a more "compassionate understanding of Dr. Peters and his economic policies during hard times". He could even joke that "Peters could hold onto a quarter until the eagle screamed!"[237]

Clara still worked by his side and offered encouragement, but the giants upon whose shoulders he had stood were no longer with him. And with Channing Tobias' death in November of 1961, Willie found himself with precious few allies who would offer support in the coming years.

"Is God there, even when he is silent, Euriah?"

It was another one of those midnight musings as a solitary figure walked the perimeter of the campus. With most of the students gone during the Christmas break, it was lonely.

"Oh, yes, my son, especially then. 'Cause He's listening very carefully, not wanting to miss one word of His child's prayers. You're not alone, boy. Not now, not ever. Me and God, we're here."

As the minutes passed, his soul was as quiet as the night.

Chapter 11 – "He listened to us far more than he ever lectured us."

February 1st, 1960: Four African American students, from North Carolina Agricultural and Technical College in Greensboro NC, enter the local Woolworth's Department Store, sit at the lunch counter, and demand to be served.

July, 1960: Harper Lee's *To Kill A Mockingbird* is published.

After serving as an assistant professor of sociology at Paine, Willie Lee Buffington received tenure during the 1961-62 academic year. It was a rare bit of stability in an increasingly unstable society, and the turbulent times broke like waves over his doorstep. For years he worked to fulfill the dream he and Euriah Simpkins saw take shape in that first library – service to an entire people consigned second class status solely for the color of their skin.

"It is the acid test if one's religion to sometimes hold on to an ideal where it seemingly doesn't pay," he said to author Beatrice Plumb in her book, *Lives that Inspire*.[238] Buffington did not say this lightly, nor in some haughty philosophical sense. He experienced it every day. His daughter, Ethel Margaret, talked about going to a white public school in Augusta. Because her father taught at Paine, her classmates resented having her in their school.[239] Dr. Clayton Calhoun, the college's president, recounted that Buffington often slept with a pistol under his pillow, facing many dangers for what he did.[240] The experience was bad enough that father and mother chose to send their son Willie Jr. to high school at the senior Buffington's alma mater, the Martha Berry School in Rome GA.

In this world that often opposed any gains in civil rights, he continued that service to others. There were times when his contributions of books were ridiculed for being of poor quality, both physically and intellectually; yet, in communities where books were scarce and education sorely lacking, they were a priceless resource. More than 100 libraries now bore witness to that fact, and the work went on unabated. The Emporia, Kansas *Gazette* reported 175 pounds of new and used books shipped in early 1962, a shared project of local Methodist Church Sunday School classes.[241]

January 31st, 1961: Students from Friendship Junior College enter McCrory's Five and Dime on Main Street in Rock Hill SC and

sit at the lunch counter. They are refused service, ordered to leave, decline to do so, and are arrested. At the hearing the following day, the Friendship Nine choose to accept 30 days at hard labor rather than post bail. It is the first time in the Civil Rights movement that "Jail, No Bail" is used as an effective strategy.

1961: John H. Griffin's *Black Like Me* is published, and tells the story of a white southerner who dyes his skin to experience first-hand the life of a black man, exposing Jim Crow brutality to a national audience.

September 30th, 1962: James Meredith is the first African American student to enroll at Ole Miss University.

April 16th, 1963: Martin Luther King, Jr. releases his "Letter From A Birmingham Jail."

June 12th, 1963: Mississippi NAACP field secretary Medgar Evers is murdered in Jackson MS.

August 28th, 1963: The March on Washington DC ("For Jobs and Freedom") occurs. Martin Luther King, Jr. delivers his "I Have A Dream" speech.

September 15th, 1963: Four young girls (Denise McNair, Cynthia Wesley, Carole Robertson, and Addie Mae Collins) are killed in the bombing of the 16th Street Baptist Church in Birmingham AL.

November 22nd, 1963: President John F. Kennedy is assassinated in Dallas TX.

Like so many in the nation, Buffington hurt with all those touched by the tragedies of the early 1960's, wept with those who lost loved ones, and rejoiced in the precious victories won at such great costs. And he worked. New libraries were established at Leary and Leesburg GA; 2000 volumes were added to the Louisville GA library; and nearly 500 books were given to Miles College.[242]

He also traveled, making his way to Daytona Beach FL in April of 1964 in his appeal for books. The local *Morning Journal* carried his photo and a story of his libraries. Drop off points for donations included the YMCA, Bethune Cookman College, and the Community Methodist

Church. He spoke at the church Monday (April 14th), and at the YMCA the next day.[243]

More than ever, "Others" mattered.

"Paine College occupies a very special place among the people and institutions that seek to level the playing field regarding issues of social justice." Silas Norman was a student at the school from 1958 to 1962, leader of the Steering Committee (the student group that spearheaded the civil rights efforts there). "I knew Mr. Buffington as a kind and wonderful personality, kind to all of us as students and committed to the work of the college".[244]

The protests rang louder, and there were high prices to pay for taking a stand against injustice.

Sometimes people listened.

January 23rd, 1964. With South Dakota as the 38th state to ratify the 24th Amendment of the US Constitution, three fourths of the states vote to outlaw the poll tax, used since Reconstruction in the South to prevent poor citizens (especially African Americans) from freely exercising their rights to vote.

July 2nd, 1964: The Civil Rights Act is passed into law, prohibiting discrimination based on race, color, religion, or national origin.

December 10th, 1964: Dr. Martin Luther King Jr. is awarded the Nobel Peace Prize, the youngest person so honored.

Sometimes they did not.

June 21st, 1964: Civil Rights workers Andrew Goodman, James Clancy and Michael Schwermer are murdered near Philadelphia MS.

Violence did not stem the tide, nor did it kill the seeds planted by men like Euriah Simpkins years before.

"I don't remember a time," noted Norman, "when we received anything less than encouragement to pursue what was considered right in human relations. That support extended through the active days of student-led protests at Paine, and continues to this day."[245]

100

The battle was joined, and it was a relentless effort. The correlative of Sir Edmund Burke's words, concerning the triumph of evil, was proven almost daily by often unrecorded acts of valor from most uncommon people: all that is necessary for justice to triumph is for good men and women to do something. Buffington was a man for that season, "a missionary of good will...who will undoubtedly have some effect in educating and developing a more enlightened interracial feeling."[246]

"He was not an advisor to the Steering Committee, but he was a part of that family unanimously offering active involvement, personal sacrifice, and spiritual support to all of our efforts," Silas Norman said.[247]

Virginia L. Jones wrote an article for the December 15th, 1963 issue of *Library Journal*. Most of the content echoed earlier works and their mapping of Buffington's life, but it was the title which stood out in these momentous times – "A Genuine Effort To Seek Truth".

Dr. Maurice Cherry returned to Paine as chaplain and reconnected with his mentor. The student went where the teacher could not, and played a central role in the organization of the Steering Committee. "Other faculty were not involved, simply because it was not their place to be involved," he remembered.[248]

The soft spoken gentleman with nerves of steel spoke fondly of both Paine College president Dr. Clayton Calhoun and "Buff" as fighters for civil rights, though they were from very different backgrounds. Calhoun wrote eloquently of the students' protests against segregation, as evidenced by his piece "Quiet Tide".

"Much fuss has been made over student demonstrations, many of the loud comments on a quiet tide. I have been related to campus movements now for thirty years, since my own admission as a freshman in 1930. I have never known a spontaneous movement to have as its base and as its aim a more quiet dignity or more sincere and devotional thought, more careful self-discipline...

"Paine students, with counsel, but without direction from faculty or administration, proceeded with dignity and continued to this hour with dignity. They approached the Mayor of Augusta with their 'concerns', were heard graciously and promised recourse to an interracial committee. The Mayor has acted in good faith, has proceeded with dispatch, but has been delayed, not defeated, by typical interpretations of 'deliberate speed.' Without defiance, then, the students on a single afternoon rode the local buses *en masse* without observing the customary segregation in seating. Eleven were arrested, bailed by local citizens who also raised a large sum for defense and appeal. On

May 18, they were convicted in City Court of disorderly conduct and fined $50.00 each, also paid by subscription. Not one single word of evidence hinted at any word, act, or gesture of disorder or discourtesy with the (protest?) of the act of selective seating. The conviction is under appeal.

"These are the simple facts. Behind them are the many hours of debate, discussion, careful weighing of values, measuring of procedures and prayerful quest for a way of dignity within Christian conscience and conduct. I believe our students and our faculty have had a most maturing experience and are more nearly one family under God than at any recent time.

"The tide has not gone out, nor does it seem to lose its quiet strength. The quiet calm of these students and the poised dignity of this community give hope that inevitable changes may not always be heralds of turbulent times…

"The hour of destiny draws near, the moment of truth. We shall have to add caution to our speed. We must move up on every front without risking the real substance of achievement by over-anxiety or frantic maneuver.

"We are so bound together in this purpose, so much a family engaged together to these ends. I have no fear at all that we shall fail. We have gained acceptance, we shall have membership, and increasingly we shall have academic excellence.

"Submitted humbly, with gratitude."[249]

When protests started in downtown Augusta, Buffington would go and mingle with the hostile crowds that often formed, to discover their intentions.

"He would return to campus, bring us together and say, 'Be careful, the crowd is out to do you harm', and would give specifics as to location, or whether they were armed. It was valuable information to have."

It is not surprising that one of Dr. Cherry's memories of Buffington was so prominently reflected in his own character. "He was an excellent counselor and a good listener. He listened to us far more than he ever lectured us."[250]

March 7th, 1965: Bloody Sunday comes to Selma AL when civil rights marchers are stopped at Pettus Bridge and a violent clash occurs.

August 10th, 1965: The Voting Rights Act is passed by Congress.

August 11th through August 17th, 1965: The Watts Riots erupt in Los Angeles CA.

September 15th, 1965: Bill Cosby co-stars with Robert Culp in television's *I Spy*. Cosby is the first African-American to appear in a starring role on the small screen.

September 24th, 1965: President Lyndon Johnson signs Executive Order 11246, legislating Affirmative Action as a vital part of awarding federal work contracts.

Though never concerned with personal recognition, Buffington had to be proud when Crozer Theological Seminary honored him as their Alumnus of the Year in October, 1965. He was the sixth recipient; Martin Luther King Jr. was the first. Willie Lee may not have made a big deal of it, but Paine College did. Dr Calhoun notified the Board of Trustees in December, and board member Dr. Allgood recommended that the honor "would appear in Paine College publications and that the Public Relations personnel of the school make this fact known to publications of our churches for their consideration".[251]

The full citation became part of the Report to the Executive Committee:

Willie Lee Buffington – Your accomplishments towards the enrichment of life have been an inspiration to countless people; among those are your fellow alumni.

You had the vision to invest ten cents into five postage stamps and watched this grow into one hundred and thirty libraries with hundreds of thousands of books, and in turn the enhancement of innumerable lives who would otherwise have been deprived of a chance to read a book.

Your libraries have been community focal points where people and books have met and lives have been changed. In them people have been gathered to help resolve the social, religious and political issues of our modern world.

We cherish your fruitful ministry.

Crozer Theological Seminary is proud to have you as an outstanding alumnus, and the Alumni Society is pleased to bestow its most coveted honor – The Alumni Achievement Award.[252]He hammered a nail into the wall and hung the citation in an inconspicuous corner of his office. Then he walked out and got back to work.

August, 1966: Ted Williams is elected to the National Baseball Hall of Fame and pointedly focuses his acceptance speech upon Negro League players denied enshrinement solely because of the color of their skin. He asks that a Veterans Committee be established to correct the injustice.

June 13th, 1967: Thurgood Marshall is the first African-American appointed to the United States Supreme Court.

Communities still came forward asking for libraries, and Willie Lee still solicited donations from across the country, specifically books of enrichment (biographies and other non-fiction) rather than textbooks. 3500 volumes were directed to Boggs Academy, a Presbyterian-sponsored school in Keysville GA, replenishing within five days what was lost in a costly fire.[253] A new library was started in Summerville SC with 3000 volumes, and additional books were supplied to Cartersville, Sylvania, Eatonton, and Pelham GA, and Bennettsville SC.[254] It was true that expansion may have slowed, but maintenance and service to some 130 libraries represented a full program. The need remained great, and people still thirsted for knowledge. Yet, for all the positive change, the laborers were still few.

Mindsets started to shift at this time, and many people began to question the need for Buffington's "little lighthouses". By the mid-1960's, many of the conditions that created the need for the Faith Cabin movement were eliminated. The Library Services Act increased funding for improved access in rural areas, and there was progress in the integration of public libraries in the region. School consolidation also had an effect, swallowing up many of the smaller facilities which housed Faith Cabin collections.[255]

Buffington sensed the changes. "The future beckons, and a larger service awaits the ministry of books."[256]

Dr. Calhoun, too, sensed the changes, and laid out to the Executive Committee of the Paine College Board of Trustees an ambitious path. Libraries would be established at churches where students could be further prepared for college. Buffington was certainly not averse to the new direction, and he was appointed the director of the outreach.

"One thing we have always wished for", Dr. Calhoun articulated, "is that students who arrive (at Paine) would have had the opportunity of more reading."

The program was established through the Colored Methodist Episcopal Church, with the Paine faculty selecting 125 books, beginning with pre-school years, which they felt students should read before entering college.[257] John and Edith Muma, of the Noyes Foundation (Jessie Smith Noyes worked for religious tolerance and racial equality), were very interested, approving a $20,000 grant for the effort in 1966, and ten libraries were organized through the cooperation of bishops and local congregations. It was understood that qualified personnel would oversee each location and handle required recordkeeping, and that the Recruitment Office at Paine would maintain contact with the libraries and participating students.

Though not reaching the large numbers of people as the Faith Cabin libraries, it did make contact with those young people who might choose to attend college.[258] According to the Report to the Board of Trustees for both 1967 and 1968, the program continued to receive favorable commentary. And Buffington remained a shining example of pursuing an education, as he received a fellowship to attend George Williams College in Chicago during the summer of 1968. The Faculty Institute on Urban Sociology addressed developing problems in urban communities in the wake of several years of civil unrest, and it was knowledge he could share with his students and colleagues at his beloved Paine.

February 8th, 1968: The Orangeburg (SC) Massacre occurs during a protest by South Carolina State University students at a segregated bowling alley.

April 4th, 1968: Dr. Martin Luther King Jr. is assassinated in Memphis TN, and riots break out in Chicago, Washington DC, Baltimore, Louisville, Kansas City and more than 150 other cities in response.

April 11th, 1968: The Civil Rights Act of 1968 is signed, and includes the Fair Housing Act, which bans discrimination in the sale, rental, and financing of housing.

June 6th, 1968: Robert F. Kennedy is assassinated after winning the California presidential primary.

November, 1968: Shirley Chisholm becomes the first African-American woman elected to Congress.

The ancient wisdom Solomon recorded in the *Book of Ecclesiastes* applied to both men and worthwhile crusades – a time to be born, and a time to die. By 1969, there was much discussion of Faith Cabin Libraries by the Board of Trustees, and it fell under the category "Clarification of Status". Two motions were put forward, seconded and passed. The first was a request to the Board of Missions for one final automobile for the work of the director. The second was to have the FCL Committee review the ministry's current status and recommend what action the Trustees and Administration should take when distributing college income to it.[259]

The concern, then, was for the money that was directed toward the work, that and nothing more. This cool approach would not have been lost on Buffington, the reduction of his life's passion to dollars and cents. Perhaps his little libraries were now viewed as unnecessary because of integration's progress and the availability of the larger public facilities to African Americans. Whatever the reasons, the 1969 Board of Trustee minutes represented the last mention of Faith Cabin Libraries in official Paine College records.

1969: The United Citizens Party is formed in South Carolina when the Democratic Party refuses to nominate African-American candidates.

1969: The W.E.B. DuBois Institute for African-American Research is founded at Harvard University.

1969: The Congressional Black Caucus is formed.

Buffington sat alone, his colleagues having exited the room soon after the meeting ended. Of all the memories that could have flooded his mind, he was surprised – and pleased – at the simplicity of those that did.

"I never tire of reading good books," one young lady called out to him, and then set to listing her favorites: Booker T. Washington's *Up From Slavery*; Edward Everett Hales's *Man Without A Country*; Nathaniel Hawthorne's *The House of Seven Gables*; Robert Louis Stevenson's *Treasure Island*; and George Eliot's *Silas Marner*.

"Through reading books," another girl called out, "I have been able to travel in many far-away lands."[260] Willie smiled quietly, remembering many such trips through the kindness of Euriah Simpkins.

"Suffer the little children to come unto me." He heard his old friend with equal measures of joy and relief, for it had been awhile since their last conversation. "Not my words exactly, but appropriate for the moment. You sad, boy?"

"Just a little used up, I think."

"The road's been long, a lot uphill, and winding enough that some folks found themselves turned around. You kept the faith."

"Not exactly your words, either." Both men laughed.

"If I have to borrow, might as well be from Jesus and Paul. A man could do worse."

"The libraries, I know they mattered," Willie said. "It's not being bitter, but I thought folks would care more..."

"Remember what you did. Is that about it, son?"

"Yes, sir."

"You got a few more miles on this road, a couple of more winding turns before you can see how things turn out. Would you trust me on that?"

Buffington sat awhile longer, letting the dim light and silence mingle, and then rose stiffly, making his way toward the door.

"I always have."

Chapter 12 – "And having done all, stand."

No one questioned Willie Lee Buffington's commitment to civil rights, or his efforts to establish and defend those rights for his black neighbors and students. But neither was he blind. In the late 1960's, well meaning and thoughtful demonstrations gave way to riots, and attitudes turned ugly. His own deep thinking led to some harsh conclusions.

"I had the deep feeling during the riot in Augusta…that Paine College had lost its purposes…goals…right to be. Irrational is about the only word that expresses the confusion and frustration." [261]

That "ugly spirit" brought with it some difficult consequences. There was a campus convocation which featured an editor from the *New York Times*. Because he was white, there was a student walkout from the chapel after his introduction by President Lucius Pitts. The speaker had a $50,000 check to present to the college, but it was not given, considering the circumstances. [262]

1969: Willie Lee Buffington receives an Honorary Doctor of Law degree from Union Baptist Seminary, Birmingham AL.

There were personal attacks as well, often from the very people for whom he had such deep regard. One was from President Calhoun, himself a fearless warrior for civil rights, and must have caused deep wounds. Dr. Maurice Cherry recalled that he and Vice-President Stuart Ganby were approached by Buffington in early 1970.

"The president said it was time for him to leave, that his only good idea had been Faith Cabin libraries, and he needed to go.

"We went to see President Calhoun, and said that we would not sit idly by and let him hurt and mistreat Buffington. The president backed off, confessing that he had rushed to judgment." [263] The intercession shored up the relationship between the two, and when Dr. Calhoun stepped down as the leader of Paine College a few months later, Buffington defended his presidency.

Buffington also had deep respect for Dr. Pitts, successor to Dr. Calhoun, and the first African American president of the college. "He had great faith in 'love as the power to redeem and reclaim', and his love for the ideals of the college motivated much of his action." There was an emphasis on accepting responsibility for freedom, and this impacted classroom work, student activities, and social life. Pitts also introduced Business courses aimed at helping more Paine students into the mainstream of economic life.

"His tenure was cut short by his death; his sacrifice for the college was great."[264]

There was one last indignity, one last painful episode to be endured in 1970, and it must have almost seemed a betrayal. One item in a list of student demands singled him out.

Item 3 was referred to the Administration with recognition that a black perspective is needed in the teaching of sociology at Paine College.[265]

Dr. Cherry and his contemporaries may have understood that Buffington came from more abject circumstances than they did, but it was lost on this new generation of students. Much as his beloved libraries were shunted aside as integration took hold, his own relevance at Paine was challenged. Though he moved from assistant to associate professor in 1972, he never felt as much a part of the college life again. In 1975 he was appointed to Faculty Emeritus status as he announced his retirement.

The packing was done, and they would be heading back to Saluda. Staring out the window, he hadn't noticed her approach. The gentle hands squeezed his shoulders, and she whispered, "Why don't you take a turn around campus before coming to bed?"

He stood and kissed her on the cheek.

"Pretty easy to read after about 45 years? Wouldn't have missed a day of it, Clara, having you by my side in this work. Just hard to believe it's at an end." His voice was hardly above a whisper.

"It mattered, Willie, to so very many, please remember that. It mattered to me."

It was humid, as only a late spring evening in Georgia can be, and distant thunder promised rain before morning. The campus was mostly empty this close to summer break. He walked slowly, looking hard at the library, classroom buildings, and dorms. How much it had all changed.

'She's right, you know, about how all those libraries mattered, that what you did changed lives for a whole generation of black folks.'

'What we did, Euriah. The four of us.'

'The Unseen Guest, you, Clara and me? Nice group of people to do business with. But there's more to it, isn't there, boy? Enough restlessness in you to shake the firmament.'

'Now it seems that I'm just used up. No great accomplishment there. Just put on the shelf like a relic from days gone by.' Had there been a passer-by, he would have noticed but a singular old man muttering sentence fragments to no one but himself.

'Remember the mudpies, Willie Lee?' He could almost see the old man smile.

'Of course I can. Greatest lesson outside Holy Scripture I was ever taught.'

'Hating your brother, remember? Now that day we talked about blood kin, but deep down we were talking way more than family. You knew that, I think, even as a child.'

'Yes, sir, think I did.'

'And you took that knowledge, and acted on it. What you did, it meant as much as Dr. King, as those folks who integrated all white high schools and colleges. You gave 'em tools, boy, thousands upon thousands of books. Gave 'em knowledge. Gave 'em education. Gave 'em hope.

'We had a dream, too. The four of us. A big dream.

'Which brings me to the reference you made about Holy Scripture. That day with those mudpies, you told me for the first time your own dream, to be a minister of the Gospel. You can do that now.'

'Got the time, that's for sure.'

'More. It's like St. Paul said, 'And having done all, stand.' Others. Remember? Always others. Wasn't ever about you. Doesn't matter what folks think. You did it all. Now, stand strong.'

The thunder was closer, and lightning flicked the dark corners of the sky where the clouds swirled.

"Storm's coming, Euriah". He completed his circle. The wind chimes on his porch swiveled in the wind. Joy bells.

'Always will, boy. You can count on it. And like that day with the mudpies, the world still needs men. Always will.'

January 25th, 1972: Shirley Chisholm is the first woman and first African-American major party candidate for the office of President of the United States.

1976: Alex Haley's *Roots: The Saga of an American Family* is published.

1977: Andrew Young, appointed by President Jimmy Carter, is the first African-American to serve as US Ambassador to the United Nations.

A young Methodist minister moved to Buffington's home turf in 1981, and began riding circuit for the small churches in Saluda and Edgefield counties. His budding friendship with the elderly man, and his

110

careful notations of what he heard and saw, provided an auspicious portrait of a life well lived.

"That whole area was struggling with how they were going to relate to each other, black and white. Willie Lee was ahead of his time, and considered by those who knew him to be in the social upheaval camp," Arthur Holt remembered. "He was somewhat harsh, but I think he had to be. An eccentric, and not overly popular with his neighbors or his family, he was an object of scorn rather than respect.[266]

"'They stand on a mountain of tradition, as they gaze fondly into the past and back boldly into the future.' That was his take on the situation, and certainly guaranteed his unpopularity."[267]

Knowing only that Buffington was a retired professor from Paine College, Holt learned about Faith Cabin Libraries much later in their relationship. His first glimpse was from the book by Beatrice Plumb, *Lives that Inspire*, in which a chapter was dedicated to the work.

"He just never talked about himself or what he had done. Willie Lee had guts, and I appreciated that."[268]

The early roots of their friendship were certainly auspicious. On Holt's first Sunday in the pulpit at Gassaway United Methodist Church, an elderly, hefty man made his way slowly down the aisle, his hair and long beard streaked with gray. He sat near the front, propped his arms on his cane, closed his eyes and seemed half asleep. But he was listening. Something about the face looked a bit Irish.

"I noticed that when I made a mistake, mispronounced a word or made an inaccurate or weak reference, he smiled. Oh, he was awake." Holt's own laughter underscored the moment. "And when he got upset about something, he would shake that cane in the air, and loudly proclaim, 'Mendacity! Utter mendacity!'"[269]

Intimidation or not, the friendship grew, and the young man could be seen driving his parishioner through the backwoods on Saluda county's dirt roads. Holt had an intimate glimpse into the places and events so crucial in shaping Willie Lee's life.

"We rode by a house that had fallen in, and only the chimney was standing. 'Stop here,' he ordered, and stared long and hard at the ruins. 'That's where I discovered America! That's my daddy's house!' Where I saw desolation, he still felt the warmth and love of childhood."[270]

When Holt and his wife were expecting their first child, the phone rang on a Saturday morning. It was Willie Lee.

"Are you sure you don't want me to get a sermon ready just in case that baby decides to come tonight?"

Holt said that maybe it wasn't such a bad idea, considering his wife had just mentioned she might be going into labor. "I really admired him, and appreciated his caring ways. Our baby girl came at 2:00AM that Sunday morning, and Willie Lee used that sermon."[271]

It was not the only time Buffington filled in, since he often preached when Holt was at another circuit location. Many people didn't attend on those particular Sundays because of who stood in the pulpit, where he had been and what he had done.

"I never knew Buffington without that beard, and I think it was part of him saying, 'Okay, you all think I'm different, so here it is."[272]

One of the sermons Willie gave as supply pastor was based on the Old Testament book of Micah, chapter 6, verse 8. It was a fitting message, from one social upheavalist to another.

...and what does the Lord require of thee, but to do justly, and to love mercy, and to walk humbly with thy God?

These were Buffington's values, the signposts on the road few men were brave enough to travel, and even fewer brave enough to complete the journey.

Reverend Holt's most perceptive observations, as he listened to the stories of childhood poverty and the long fight for civil rights, concerned that path his friend had chosen. "I didn't ever think Willie Lee woke up one morning and said 'I'm going to right a wrong.' No, one man, Euriah Simpkins, helped him transcend his time. And his love for that one man led Buffington to do what he did, paying Simpkins back, honoring him by being a good man. It was, I always thought, a labor of love more than a labor of justice."[273]

Watching young Holt grow and mature in his calling certainly brought a measure of joy into Buffington's life, and sparked memories of pastorates he had served as a member of the North Georgia Methodist Church Conference. While at Grovetown in 1966, they were attempting to merge with the all-black Georgia Conference, and he remained a strong voice for integrating the church.[274]

Buffington told of another episode, this at a church near Augusta. "I had one member who had been elected Chairman of the Board of Stewards. When I came, he resigned. He didn't tell me why, but I learned later that he said he had other things more important to do than to listen to a preacher on Sunday mornings who didn't have anything more worthwhile to do during the week than to teach a bunch of 'niggers'. I just dropped it at that and found me a young man to serve as Chairman. That's the only objection I encountered out there."[275]

Buffington had given much, worked for a cause much greater than himself, and played a role in changing the social landscape of the south. For all that, Willie was still a man well acquainted with grief. He lost his mother at such a young age that memories of her were but fleeting images. His grandmother, who had given him his foundation in the Christian faith, followed not many years later. The loss of Euriah Simpkins affected him deeply, coming when he was a young man who felt the weight of his burdens more profoundly than most. His father, Dr. B.E. Geer, Dr. E.C. Peters and Miss Emma C.W. Gray had passed from his life as well.

None of this prepared him for the loss of his beloved wife. Clara had been by his side for more than 45 years, birthing two children and scores of libraries, changing diapers and sorting books for hopeful multitudes in crossroad communities across South Carolina and Georgia. Her laughter filled his soul and lightened his load. Her love made even the darkest days bearable, and promised a sunrise filled with hope. But her big heart grew weary as she gave unselfishly, until there was simply no more to give. She passed away on October 7th, 1983. An unreferenced obituary lauded her.

"Clara shared with her husband a vision to raise their black brothers and sisters out of poverty and improve their education. She was her husband's partner in the establishment of 139 Faith Cabin Libraries in the South so that black children in rural areas could have books for their education. Her attitude in race relations was years ahead of its time."[276]

"Mrs. Buffington was a remarkable woman in her own right," Reverend Holt said, "very much a partner in the Faith Cabin Library work, very much in favor of what her husband was doing. She was a sweet lady, and Willie loved her deeply."

Called on to preach her funeral, Holt did a fine job, and Buffington complimented him on his eulogy. The young man deflected his praise, mumbling something like 'just doing my job'. It proved a poor choice of words, though the bereaved husband said nothing until the two stood alone following the morning service the following Sunday.

Brandishing his cane, Willie said, "When you have just buried a man's wife, *you don't ever* say you were just doing your job!" Wise beyond his years, young Holt concurred. "You're right."

Then, "I embraced him, and he didn't resist at all."[277]

August 30th, 1983: Guion Bluford is the first African-American astronaut to go into space.

November 2nd, 1983: President Reagan signs the bill establishing a federal holiday to honor Dr. Martin Luther King Jr. It is first celebrated as a national holiday in 1986.

Willie seemed alone and lost. He continued his work as a supply pastor for the county's small rural churches through the Saluda Ministerial Association, and filled his hours as a member of both the local Civitan Club, the Saluda County Council on Aging, and the Saluda County Historical Society. Slowly, however, his own health began to fail. His heart, like Clara's, was giving out. A pacemaker held the condition in check, and for a while Buffington's sister-in-law, Ida Jones, helped to care for him at home. "Once you taste the waters of Red Bank Creek," Willie often said, "you want to come back here to die."[278]

November, 1989: *Freedom Bound: A History of America's Civil Rights Movement*, by Robert Weisbrot, is published.

Buffington's final years were spent with his son, Bill, and it was in a Spartanburg hospital where Holt met with his friend for the last time, in August of 1989.

"How are you?"

"Slow". He still had his long hair and beard. His voice grew stronger as he said, "You're the one I want to preach my funeral."

Two weeks later, Holt did just that, telling the story of a man who gave all he had and changed so many lives. He typed his comments, because one of Buffington's granddaughters was deaf. Along with everyone else, she would share in the eulogy.[279]

"I felt privileged to tell his story in the community where he came from, telling it to family and neighbors who did not realize the significance of all that he had done. I wasn't sure it would be told otherwise, and I wanted everyone to hear it, especially those who had never totally accepted what he did with the Faith Cabin Libraries." Several family members commented after the service that they knew nothing of what he had done in this regard.

"This guy, who maybe they didn't like too much, had helped bring about a tremendous change is society and had done wonderful things. I was hoping to instill a sense of pride, of celebration, but perhaps that is for the next generation to discover."[280]

Buffington's story, though, still finds its way into every pastorate Holt serves. A very special sermon, "The 5K Buffet" resonates with the heart and soul of the boy gifted with such uncommon love.

"When I mention Jesus feeding the 5000+ by blessing and multiplying another poor boy's meager gift of five little loaves of bread and two small fish, it begs comparison to Willie Lee buying five two-cent postage stamps with that single dime in his pocket and starting the Faith Cabin Library movement. Jesus multiplies loaves and fishes, or whatever we give Him. Our part is to give Him what we have and who we are. Willie Lee blazed a trail, and more needs to be made of what he did."[281]

While a supply pastor, Willie spoke from the pulpit at Tignall (GA) United Methodist Church in March of 1974, and presented a sermon entitled "Nominal Christian or Zealous Disciple". He said that "the hand that can do no humble thing for man will do even less for God. The doors we open each day decide the lives we live."[282] Through books, he opened passageways to better lives for generations of poor African-American neighbors long denied the chance of an education. "Nominal" never figured into who he was, simply because he walked with Euriah Simpkins, who urged him to be a man because "the world needs men".

God knows, it still does.

Buffington plot. Trinity Lutheran Church Cemetery, Saluda SC.
Photo taken by author.

Afterword

Julius Rosenwald and Willie Lee Buffington

They were the most unlikely people to have anything in common. The one, Julius Rosenwald, was of Jewish heritage, a middle class Midwesterner from Chicago. The other, Willie Buffington, was the son of a poor sharecropper from South Carolina, whose Christian roots stretched back generations. The more privileged Rosenwald ended his formal education at age 15, choosing to become an apprentice in the clothing industry. With hard work and a gifted intellect, he became president of Sears and Roebuck Company and amassed great personal wealth. Engulfed by poverty, Buffington was forced to leave school after the eighth grade to work and help support his family. Yet, he embraced education, graduating from high school at age 26, then earning college and graduate degrees and becoming a college professor. Rosenwald was nearly 70 when he died in 1932, just as Buffington, age 24, rejoiced in finding the work that would guide his life.

What both men passionately shared was a disdain for injustice and racial prejudice. Rosenwald's personal and public philanthropies totaled nearly $70 million, and much of the Rosenwald Fund was earmarked for the educational and economic well-being of African Americans after he visited the south. Buffington's life work, establishing Faith Cabin Libraries in small rural communities (often located near schools or in school buildings made possible by the Rosenwald Fund), made books readily available to southern blacks for the first time, and made attaining an education a real possibility. Both men read, and were profoundly affected by, Booker T. Washington's *Up From Slavery*. Rosenwald had the privilege of meeting that distinguished leader in Chicago. Both Rosenwald and Buffington, in their own ways, kept the subject of race relations and racial equality in front of the American people. Rosenwald was concerned with discrimination against any race, religion or creed, so highly did he regard American democracy. Buffington genuinely (and rightly) believed that no one could profess to be a follower of Jesus Christ and harbor hatred and prejudice toward his or her fellow man. Rosenewald's own Jewish heritage was filled with oppression throughout history, and it was something he fought to end. Buffington's friendship with Euriah Simpkins led to a similar vow, that oppression against his African American friends and neighbors would not go unchallenged in the south where Jim Crow laws controlled everything but conscience.

117

One man bridged the generational gap between Rosenwald and Buffington – Dr. Will Alexander. The founder of the Committee on Interracial Cooperation during the terrible race riots in the summer of 1919 served as a Rosenwald Foundation trustee from 1930 through 1948. There was a powerful link forged between Chicago and Atlanta that time did not weaken. Alexander also corresponded with Buffington during the early years of the Faith Cabin Library movement, and the two men met on the campus of Paine College in Augusta GA during the 1930's. Much as Alexander had influenced the work of the Rosenwald Foundation, he also helped to guide the young southerner during his formative years of interracial work, certainly strengthening those efforts in a region of "separate but equal" mentality.

Rosenwald's business model for his fund was ingenious: the monies must be spent within 25 years of the establishment of the Foundation. Effectively, the Rosenwald Fund ceased in the late 1940's, fulfilling the founder's directive of putting the world in good shape for those who followed. There was no time to build a bureaucracy. Buffington's business model was a single word, "Others", which adorned a wall in every library he built. He wrote letters of supplication long into the night after finishing his shift at the Edgefield Cotton Mill (and later after teaching his classes at Benedict and Paine colleges), asking for donations of books, with the only provision that the freight be pre-paid. That way, his costs were reduced to his and his wife's labor to cull and sort the books when they arrived, and to make sure the volumes were delivered to the designated locations. Like Rosenwald's, the plan was brilliant in its simplicity, and worked effectively.

Communities took pride in the Rosenwald schools and Faith Cabin Libraries, and both served as centers for local activities. Most importantly, they forged a necessary link in the fight against African-American illiteracy in the rural south. More than $4 million was designated from the Rosenwald Fund for school building construction, with another $860,000 for library services and books. Conservative estimates of books donated to Buffington's libraries exceeded 100,000.

The contributions of Julius Rosenwald have faded from public view in the decades since the fund and foundation named for him came to an end. Those of Willie Buffington have never been fully acknowledged, despite his having given all of his adult life to bringing opportunities through literacy to citizens in scores of African-American communities. Together they helped bring about a generation of people who could read, and whose access to books and education opened doors to a whole new world. They lived their convictions at a time when the world needed men, as Euriah Simpkins so eloquently stated, and good men need to be remembered.

Following are testimonials to the impact of the Faith Cabin Libraries, some from the very people who used them and embarked upon incredible journeys.

"I knew Mr. Buffington before I was enrolled in elementary school. He visited our home and collected books for Aiken SC. One never sees Mr. Buffington unless one sees books. He still believes what his grandmother taught him, and he lives daily by the faith that 'God makes miracles.'" -Sheslonia Greene[283]

"What I think was the most remarkable thing about Mr. Buffington was his racial attitude, and his desire to recognize the Negro teacher to whom he owed so much, by making books available to Negro children. His sense of social justice was really remarkable."
-Charlotte Templeton, Librarian, Greenville SC Public Library[284]

"It is refreshing to discover a person of your convictions and ambitions, who in a pragmatic world finds himself moving in a spiritual atmosphere, saturated with moral steadfastness."
-Jesse O. Thomas Sr., Field Director, National Urban League[285]

"I have always been interested in Willie's work and have helped him as much as possible. Due to the high cost of living, the rates for a room at the motels, the price of food, and his limited amount of money, I remain at home more now." -Clara R. Buffington[286]

"The movement was the largest private, community-based movement in the Southeast (and perhaps the entire country) involved in establishing library collections for African-Americans, at a time when they were almost completely excluded from public libraries in the Southeast." -Dr. Robert Williams, Professor Emeritus USC[287]

"Anything that can be done to facilitate the progress of his constructive program will be a lasting investment in improved minds and encouragement of people who greatly need such help." -Dr. Channing Tobias, National Council YMCA[288]

"I have spent four years at Paine College and Mr. Buffington has taught me to rely upon the fourth chapter of *St. Luke*, verses 18 and 19 for

119

inspiration and courage. He is a man of faith and has a deal of respect for others. He is a wonderful counselor, sympathetic and very humble." -Pierre Shaumbra[289]

"To my knowledge, Mr. Buffington has done more for the Negro school libraries in Georgia than any other person or organization. He and his family are humble, religious, and stand up to be counted whenever there is a principle involved." -Mildred Floyd Southwood[290]

"I know of no more unique interracial enterprise being conducted anywhere in the South, nor, of any enterprise that is yielding larger returns than this work." -Dr. E.C. Peters, President, Paine College[291]

"Mr. Buffington, in his efforts to develop these libraries, deserves the support of people who are sympathetic with this who desire better human relations." -Dr. W.W. Alexander, Commission on Interracial Cooperation.[292]

"Mr. Buffington has used his education as a southern country preacher to teach others of his race to be liberal toward Negroes. I have worked on committee with him and he stands for what he thinks to be the right thing at all times." -George Caldwell[293]

"Mr. Buffington is the least race conscious person I have ever met. I knew him before he quit the cotton mill to go back to school. He is one person who has shown most growth in correcting social attitudes that were undesirable. He is decent, right, democratic, and has moral courage." -William L. Graham[294]

Buffington at Benedict College.
Courtesy Una Roberts Lawrence Papers,
Southern Baptist Historical Library and Archives, Nashville TN.

Appendix – "Little lighthouses."

Following is a list of the Faith Cabin Libraries by date of founding. The 120 libraries appearing here have been verified multiple times through source materials.

'Name', 'School', 'Place' and 'Donor(s)' suggested themselves as identifiers after the first 25 libraries were catalogued. Indeed, only two unit names were missing. 'Notes' was added to cite interesting facts available. Later, unit names in particular became more difficult to find, but in deference to consistency of form, identifiers were left blank rather than eliminated.

It is hoped that this brief factual evidence will sketch a clear portrait of each library and its special place in the community.

## and Name	1-Lizzie Koon Unit. Established December 31, 1932.
School	Plum Branch Rosenwald School.
Place	Saluda; Saluda County SC.
Donor(s)	St. Mark Methodist Episcopal Church; Harlem NY. 1600 volumes.
Notes	Named in honor of Buffington's mother.

## and Name	2-Annie Bodie Unit. Established 1934.
School	Ridge Hill Rosenwald School (built with WPA labor).
Place	Ridge Spring; Saluda County SC.
Donor(s)	General contributions. 2000 volumes.
Notes	Named in honor of Buffington's step-mother.

## and Name	3-L.H. King Unit. Established 1935.
School	Drayton Street School.
Place	Newberry; Newberry County SC.
Donor(s)	Surplus from the Annie Bodie Unit. 2200 volumes.
Notes	Named in honor of the pastor of St. Mark Methodist Episcopal Church, Harlem, NY.

## and Name	4-Catherine Degen Unit. Established 1936.
School	Anderson County Training School.
Place	Pendleton; Anderson County SC.
Donor(s)	General contributions. 2400 volumes.
Notes	Named in honor of Buffington's New York benefactor and friend.

## and Name	5-Bessie Drew Unit. Established 1936.
School	Chapman Grove Rosenwald School.
Place	Pelzer; Anderson/Greenville counties SC.
Donor(s)	General contributions. 2600 volumes.
Notes	Named in honor of the editor of *The Workman* magazine.

## and Name	6-Oberlin College Unit. Established 1937.
School	Seneca Junior College.
Place	Seneca; Oconee County SC.
Donor(s)	Oberlin College (OH) students/faculty. 4000 volumes.
Notes	Out of service by 1950.

## and Name	7-Abraham Lincoln Unit. Established 1937.
School	Fountain Inn Negro School.
Place	Fountain Inn; Greenville County SC.
Donor(s)	Books collected by Isaac Diller, Springfield IL. 2800 volumes.
Notes	Diller was the only person living at that time photographed with Abraham Lincoln.

## and Name	8-Hanover-Dartmouth Unit. Established 1938.
School	Simpson Junior High School.
Place	Easley; Greenville County SC.
Donor(s)	Christian Union of Hanover NH, and Dartmouth College. 3000 volumes.
Notes	400 textbooks and an encyclopedia set were reserved for Adult Education.

## and Name	9-B.E. Geer Unit. Established 1938.
School	Geer-Rosenwald School.
Place	Belton; Anderson County SC.
Donor(s)	Readers of Beatrice Plumb's "Joy Bells Ringing". 1800 volumes.
Notes	Geer was president of Furman University when Buffington attended.

## and Name	10-Iowa City Unit. Established 1938.
School	Bettis Academy.
Place	Trenton; Edgefield County SC.
Donor(s)	Iowa City (IA) Ministerial Association. 8000 volumes.
Notes	Concrete blocks for the library were made onsite.

## and Name	11-Albert H. Stamm Unit. Established 1938.
School	Inman Negro High School.
Place	Inman; Spartanburg County SC.
Donor(s)	Books collected by Albert Stamm. 1800 volumes.
Notes	Stamm, a disabled World War I veteran, collected four tons of books.

## and Name	12-Elyria (OH) Unit. Established 1938.
School	Edgefield Academy.
Place	Edgefield; Edgefield County SC.
Donor(s)	Elyria (OH) Church groups. 1600 volumes.
Notes	Truck driver who delivered the books moved the Buffington household goods to Crozer Theological Seminary.

## and Name	13-George A. Brown Unit. Established 1938.
School	Edgefield County Training School.
Place	Johnston; Edgefield County SC.
Donor(s)	General contributions.1800 volumes.
Notes	

## and Name	14-Decatur Unit. Established 1939.
School	Batesburg Negro High School.
Place	Batesburg; Lexington County SC.
Donor(s)	Mrs. S.D. Beavers, Decatur IN. 2000 volumes.
Notes	School and library were destroyed by fire in 1950.

## and Name	15-Mt. Gretna Unit. Established 1940.
School	Saluda Rosenwald School.
Place	Saluda; Saluda County SC.
Donor(s)	Mt. Gretna (PA) Players. 2400 volumes.
Notes	Margaret Hansfield organized donations through this drama company.

## and Name	16-Hobby Lobby Unit. Established 1940.
School	Lexington Rosenwald School.
Place	Lexington; Lexington County SC.
Donor(s)	Listeners of Dave Inman's Hobby Lobby Radio Show. 2200 volumes.
Notes	Buffington was a guest speaker on the show his first year at Crozer.

## and Name	17-Lucy Harris Unit. Established 1940.
School	Georgetown Negro High School; Howard High School.
Place	Georgetown; Georgetown County SC.
Donor(s)	Hobby Lobby listeners; "Joy Bells Ringing" readers. 2000 volumes.
Notes	

## and Name	18-
School	Jamestown Negro School. Library established 1940.
Place	Jamestown; Georgetown County SC.
Donor(s)	Jamestown NY citizens. 1500 volumes.
Notes	Jamestown citizens were Hobby Lobby listeners and "Joy Bells Ringing" readers.

## and Name	19-Euriah W. Simpkins Unit. Established 1940.
School	Boughknight's School.
Place	Johnston; Edgefield County SC.
Donor(s)	Hobby Lobby listeners and "Joy Bells Ringing" readers. 1200 volumes.
Notes	Named in honor of Buffington's long-time mentor and friend.

## and Name	20-Queen's Village Unit. Established 1941.
School	Marlboro County Training School.
Place	Bennettsville; Marlboro County SC.
Donor(s)	Queens' Village (NY) Baptist Church. 10,000 volumes.
Notes	The campaign slogan was "10,000 Books In 10 Weeks."

## and Name	21-Rockford (IL) Unit. Established 1941.
School	Aiken Negro School.
Place	Aiken; Aiken County SC.
Donor(s)	Mrs. Dorcas Hall collected books through local Lutheran churches. 1200 volumes.
Notes	

## and Name	22-Harry A. Mackey Unit. Established 1941.
School	Sterling High School.
Place	Greenville; Greenville County SC.
Donor(s)	Mrs. Mary Rose Collins and the Matinee Musical Club of Philadelphia (PA). 3200 volumes.
Notes	

## and Name	23-M.W. Buffington Unit. Established 1941.
School	Elisha School.
Place	Silverstreet; Newberry County SC.
Donor(s)	General contributions. 1100 volumes.
Notes	Named in honor of Buffington's father, who often helped in this work.

## and Name	24-
School	Whitmire Negro School. Library established 1941.
Place	Whitmire; Newberry County SC.
Donor(s)	General contributions. 1200 volumes.
Notes	

## and Name	25-
School	B.B. Leitzsey Community School. Library established 1941.
Place	Newberry; Newberry County SC.
Donor(s)	General contributions. 1000 volumes.
Notes	The Mt.Bethel-Garmany rural community provided local support.

## and Name	26-
School	Mt. Carmel Rosenwald School. Library established 1942.
Place	Owings; Laurens County SC.
Donor(s)	General contributions. 1100 volumes.
Notes	

## and Name	27-
School	Gray Court Negro School. Library established 1942.
Place	Gray Court; Laurens County SC.
Donor(s)	General contributions. 2200 volumes.
Notes	

## and Name	28-
School	Chesnee Negro School. Library established 1942.
Place	Chesnee; Spartanburg County SC.
Donor(s)	General contributions. 1200 volumes.
Notes	

## and Name	29-
School	Camp Liberty High School. Library established 1942.
Place	Jenkinsville; Fairfield County SC.
Donor(s)	General contributions. 1800 volumes.
Notes	

## and Name	30-
School	New Bethel High School. Library established 1943.
Place	Woodruff; Spartanburg County SC.
Donor(s)	General contributions. 2500 volumes.
Notes	

## and Name	31-Community Library. Established 1944.
School	
Place	Augusta; Richmond County GA.
Donor(s)	General contributions. Several thousand volumes.
Notes	Now the Wallace Branch of the Public Library system.

## and Name	32-
School	McDuffie County Training School. Library established 1944.
Place	Thomason; McDuffie County GA.
Donor(s)	5th Grade, Friends School, Baltimore MD. 1800 volumes.
Notes	R.L. Norris, school principal.

## and Name	33-
School	Starks School of Theology, Benedict College. Books added 1944.
Place	Columbia; Richland County SC.
Donor(s)	Books donated from libraries of retired/deceased ministers. Several hundred volumes.
Notes	Dr. Starks hired Buffington to come to Benedict College.

## and Name	34-North Indiana Unit. Established 1944.
School	Swainsboro High & Industrial School.
Place	Swainsboro; Emanuel County GA.
Donor(s)	Northern Indiana Women's Society of Christian Service. 2700 volumes.
Notes	D.D. Boston, school principal. Library dedicated April 1, 1949.

## and Name	35-
School	T.J. Elder High School. Library established 1944.
Place	Sandersville; Washington County GA.
Donor(s)	Indiana Women's Society of Christian Service. 2800 volumes.
Notes	Julian D. Davis, school principal; S.E. Butler, librarian.

## and Name	36-
School	Jefferson County Training School. Library established 1945.
Place	Louisville; Jefferson County GA.
Donor(s)	Troy NY Women's Society of Christian Service. 3200 volumes.
Notes	W.E. Price, school principal. Library dedicated May 24, 1948.

## and Name	37-
School	Wadley Negro High School; Carver Elementary School. Library established 1945.
Place	Wadley; Jefferson County GA.
Donor(s)	Rockford IL Men's Bible Class. 2100 volumes.
Notes	Q.E. Parker, school principal.

## and Name	38-Dublin Community Library. Established 1945.
School	Laurens County Training School; Oconee High School.
Place	Dublin; Laurens County GA.
Donor(s)	NY Conference Women's Society of Christian Service. 3000 volumes.
Notes	Charles W. Manning, school principal; Katherine Gray, Jeanes Supervisor.

## and Name	39-Community Center. Established 1945.
School	Warren Jr. High School; Southwest Elementary School.
Place	Devereux; Warren County GA.
Donor(s)	Southern IL Women's Society of Christian Service. 3000 volumes.
Notes	A.M. Benson, school principal. Library dedicated October 31, 1948.

## and Name	40-
School	Abbeville Negro School; Neapolis Street Elementary School. Library established 1945.
Place	Abbeville; Wilcox County GA.
Donor(s)	Central PA Women's Society of Christian Service. 2800 volumes.
Notes	K.N. Colclough, school principal; Mrs. J.R. Dennis, Jeanes Supervisor.

## and Name	41-
School	Putman County Training School; Eatonton Negro High School. Library established 1946.
Place	Eatonton; Putman County GA.
Donor(s)	Ohio Conference Women's Society of Christian Service. 3000 volumes.
Notes	W.N. McGlockton, school principal. Library dedicated October 7, 1949.

## and Name	42-
School	Eureka High School. Library established 1946.
Place	Ashburn; Turner County GA.
Donor(s)	Newark NJ Conf. Women's Society of Christian Service. 4000 volumes.
Notes	Hodge King, school principal. Library dedicated February 11, 1949.

## and Name	43-
School	Seminole County Training School. Library established 1946.
Place	Donaldsonville; Seminole County GA.
Donor(s)	New Jersey Conf. Women's Society of Christian Service. 2400 volumes.
Notes	R.D. Romlison, school principal. Library dedicated May 15, 1950.

## and Name	44-
School	Peabody High School. Library established 1946.
Place	Eastman; Dodge County GA.
Donor(s)	Indianapolis IN District Women's Society of Christian Service. 2800 volumes.
Notes	St. Elmo Morgan, school principal.

## and Name	45-Genessee Conference Unit. Established 1947.
School	Cartersville Community Library.
Place	Cartersville; Bartow County GA.
Donor(s)	Genessee Conference Women's Society of Christian Service. 3600 volumes.
Notes	Sadie Wheeler, Jeanes Supervisor. Library dedicated November 13, 1948.

## and Name	46-
School	Cleveland Consolidated school for Negroes; Oak Springs Elementary School. Library established 1947.
Place	Cleveland; White County GA.
Donor(s)	Alpha Delta Class, Poughkeepsie NY. 1100 volumes.
Notes	Henry Keane, school principal.

## and Name	47- Rip Van Winkle Library. Established 1947.
School	Rural Christian Center.
Place	Haddock; Jones County GA.
Donor(s)	George W. Bagley, Catskills NY. 5000 volumes.
Notes	Mrs. B.N. Mayes, librarian; Marie Collins, Jeanes Supervisor.

## and Name	48-
School	Wilkinson County Training School; Gordon Negro School. Library established 1947.
Place	Gordon; Wilkinson County GA.
Donor(s)	General contributions. 1000 volumes.
Notes	Walter Z. Thomas, school principal; Tommie C. Calhoun, Jeanes Supervisor.

## and Name	49-Coronet Unit.
School	Baxley Negro Training School. Library established 1948.
Place	Baxley; Appling County GA.
Donor(s)	Readers of Herman Styler's 1947 *Coronet* article. 10,000 volumes.
Notes	M.E. Cooks, school principal. Library dedicated May 1, 1949.

## and Name	50-
School	Howard-Warner High School; Coweta Central High School. Library established 1948.
Place	Newnan; Coweta County GA.
Donor(s)	Erie NY Conference Women's Society of Christian Service. 3000 volumes.
Notes	F.A. Dodson, school principal.

## and Name	51-War Heroes Memorial Unit. Established 1948.
School	Lithonia Negro High School; Brice Street High and Elementary Schools.
Place	Lithonia; DeKalb County GA.
Donor(s)	Listeners of "Ted Malone, Westinghouse Story Teller" Radio Show. 2800 volumes.
Notes	Coy E. Flagg, school principal.

## and Name	52-
School	R.J. Backwell Memorial High School. Library established May 22, 1949.
Place	Elberton; Elbert County GA.
Donor(s)	Illinois Conference Women's Society of Christian Service. 3800 volumes.
Notes	Mrs. W.A. Payton guided donor efforts. James Hawes, school principal.

## and Name	53-
School	Jeffersonville Vocational Negro School. Library established and dedicated April 24, 1949.
Place	Jeffersonville; Twiggs County GA.
Donor(s)	General contributions. 3600 volumes.
Notes	A.M. Fields and W.E. West, school principals.

## and Name	54-
School	George Washington Carver High School. Library established and dedicated May 25, 1949.
Place	Douglas; Coffee County GA.
Donor(s)	NY East Conf. Women's Society of Christian Service. 6000 volumes.
Notes	Joseph Murray, school principal.

## and Name	55-
School	Hart County Training School; Hartwell Negro High School. Library established August 12, 1949.
Place	Hartwell; Hart County GA.
Donor(s)	General contributions. 2400 volumes.
Notes	Leonard N. Rogers, school principal.

## and Name	56-Community Library. Established August 27, 1949.
School	
Place	St. Matthews; Calhoun County SC.
Donor(s)	General contributions. 1500 volumes.
Notes	Now part of the public library system.

## and Name	57-
School	Quitman Negro School; Brooks County High/Training School; Washington Street High School. Library established 1949.
Place	Quitman; Brooks County GA.
Donor(s)	General contributions. 6000 volumes.
Notes	C.W. Rutherford, school principal. Library dedicated May 15, 1950.

## and Name	58-
School	McRae Negro School; Central High School. Library established September 12, 1950.
Place	McRae; Telfair County GA.
Donor(s)	General contributions.
Notes	Robert F. Jackson, school principal.

## and Name	59-
School	Holsey Institute (Christian Methodist Episcopal Church secondary school). Library established September 30, 1950.
Place	Cordele; Crisp County GA.
Donor(s)	Rock River Conf. Women's Society of Christian Service. 1000 volumes.
Notes	Mrs. Rouse T. Hollis, school principal.

## and Name	60-
School	Library established October 4, 1950.
Place	Toccoa; Stephens County GA.
Donor(s)	Detroit MI Conference Women's Society of Christian Service.
Notes	

## and Name	61-Faith Cabin Library Unit. Established January 1, 1951.
School	Homerville Elementary and High Schools.
Place	Homerville; Clinch County GA.
Donor(s)	Belvedere IL Educational Association. 6000 volumes.
Notes	Ellis Whitaker, school principal.

## and Name	62-
School	J.P. Carr High and Elementary Schools. Library established January 6, 1951.
Place	Conyers; Rockdale County GA.
Donor(s)	Peninsula Conf. Women's Society of Christian Service. 3000 volumes.
Notes	George L. Edwards, school principal.

## and Name	63-
School	Crawfordville Negro High School; Murden High and Elementary Schools. Library established April 26, 1951.
Place	Crawfordville; Taliferro County GA.
Donor(s)	Detroit Conference Women's Society of Christian Service.
Notes	Harry S. King, school principal.

## and Name	64-
School	Screven County Training School; Central High School. Library established April 29, 1951.
Place	Sylvania; Screven County GA.
Donor(s)	Redland CA Kiwanis Club. 4800 volumes.
Notes	J.T. Lacy, school principal.

## and Name	65-
School	Wayne County Training School. Library established October 9, 1951.
Place	Jesup; Wayne County GA.
Donor(s)	Port Huron MI District Women's Society of Christian Service.
Notes	Frank Robinson, school principal.

## and Name	66-
School	Lumber City Negro Elementary School. Library established November 6, 1951.
Place	Lumber City; Telfair County GA.
Donor(s)	CPC, Washington Diocese.
Notes	Elmo Green Jr., school principal.

## and Name	67-
School	J.F. Boddie High School; Carver High School. Library established December 17, 1951.
Place	Milledgeville; Baldwin County GA.
Donor(s)	General contributions.
Notes	Joseph M. Graham, school principal.

## and Name	68-
School	Hooper-Renwick High School; Lawrenceville Negro School. Library established March 15, 1952.
Place	Lawrenceville; Gwinnett County GA.
Donor(s)	General contributions.
Notes	R.L. Hightower, school principal.

## and Name	69-
School	Ralph Bunche High School. Library established May 26, 1952.
Place	Woodbine; Camden County GA.
Donor(s)	General contributions.
Notes	S.D. Tarver, school principal.

## and Name	70-
School	Ocilla Negro Industrial High School. Library established 1952-53.
Place	Ocilla; Irwin County GA.
Donor(s)	Readers of Emma C. Gray's "A Man and His Ministry of Books".
Notes	Alphonso Owens, school principal.

## and Name	71-
School	Ballard-Hudson High School. Library established September 23, 1953.
Place	Macon; Bibb County GA.
Donor(s)	Youth of Newburgh District, Ellenville NY
Notes	R.J. Martin, school principal.

## and Name	72-
School	Walker High School. Library established January 5, 1954.
Place	Ludowici; Long County GA.
Donor(s)	Women's Auxiliary, Trinity Episcopal Church, Williamsport PA.
Notes	E.J. Junior, school principal.

## and Name	73-
School	W.A. Fountain High School. Library established January 9, 1954.
Place	Forest Park; Clayton County GA.
Donor(s)	Readers of *Guideposts* Magazine article on Faith Cabin Library.
Notes	M.D. Roberts, school principal.

## and Name	74-
School	Hephizbah Consolidated School; Floyd Graham Elementary School. Library established January 27, 1954.
Place	Hephizbah; Richmond County GA.
Donor(s)	Listeners of Dupont's Cavalcade of America's "Uncle Eury's Dollar".
Notes	Hubert Wilson, school principal.

## and Name	75-
School	Hubbard High School. Library established April 15, 1954.
Place	Forsythe; Monroe County GA.
Donor(s)	Quakers.
Notes	S.E. Hubbard, school principal.

## and Name	76-
School	Crawford County Training School; Roberta Consolidated Negro School. Library established October 16, 1954.
Place	Roberta; Crawford County GA.
Donor(s)	General contributions.
Notes	E.E. Owens, school principal.

## and Name	77-
School	Mitchell County Training School; Pelham Consolidated Negro School. Library established November 11, 1954.
Place	Pelham; Mitchell County GA.
Donor(s)	General contributions.
Notes	Beaufort C. Maudeville, school principal.

## and Name	78-
School	Mary Johnson High School; Heard County Training School. Library established January 8, 1955.
Place	Franklin; Heard County GA.
Donor(s)	General contributions.
Notes	Felton J. Rausby, school principal; ____ Nunn, librarian.

## and Name	79-
School	Marion County Colored School; Buena Vista Negro High School. Library established January 23, 1955.
Place	Buena Vista; Marion County GA.
Donor(s)	General contributions.
Notes	Casilo D. Hughes, school principal.

## and Name	80-
School	Washington High School. Library established April 9, 1955.
Place	Blakely; Early County GA.
Donor(s)	General contributions.
Notes	C.E. Stanley, school principal.

## and Name	81-
School	Miller County/Bethel Training School; Colquitt Consolidated School. Library established May 14, 1955.
Place	Colquitt; Miller County GA.
Donor(s)	General contributions.
Notes	James E. Merritt, school principal.

## and Name	82-
School	Charlton County/Bethune Training School. Library established June 2, 1955.
Place	Folkston; Charlton County GA.
Donor(s)	General contributions.
Notes	Mrs. Robert DeLoache Jr., school principal.

## and Name	83-
School	Lincolnton County Negro Training School. Library established December 10, 1955.
Place	Lincolnton; Lincoln County GA.
Donor(s)	General contributions.
Notes	Welcome Moson, school principal.

## and Name	84-
School	Burke County Negro Training School; Waynesboro High/Industrial School. Library established January 28, 1956.
Place	Waynesboro; Burke County GA.
Donor(s)	General contributions.
Notes	R.E. Blakeney, school principal.

## and Name	85-
School	Atkinson County Training School. Library established April 21,1956.
Place	Pearson; Atkinson County GA.
Donor(s)	General contributions.
Notes	Charles Rawls, school principal.

## and Name	86-
School	Booker High School. Library established August 28, 1956.
Place	Barnesville; Lamar County GA.
Donor(s)	General contributions.
Notes	E.P. Roberts, school principal.

## and Name	87-
School	Liberty County Training School. Library established May 2, 1956.
Place	Midway; Liberty County GA.
Donor(s)	General contributions.
Notes	Samuel L. Smith, school principal.

## and Name	88-
School	A.S. Clark High School. Library established October 13, 1956.
Place	Cordele; Crisp County GA.
Donor(s)	General contributions.
Notes	L.W. Coleman, school principal.

## and Name	89-
School	Jasper County Training School. Library established December 8, 1956.
Place	Monticello; Jasper County GA.
Donor(s)	Pittsburgh PA Conference Women's Society of Christian Service, "Book Sharing Project".
Notes	A.R. Payne, school principal; Dorothy Cochran, librarian.

## and Name	90-
School	Washington Consolidated School; Grady County Consolidated School. Library established March 19, 1957.
Place	Cairo; Grady County GA.
Donor(s)	General contributions.
Notes	Daniel T. Grant, school principal.

## and Name	91-
School	Effingham County Training School; Springfield Central High School. Library established May 11, 1957.
Place	Springfield; Effingham County GA.
Donor(s)	General contributions.
Notes	C.A. Wiggins, school principal.

## and Name	92-
School	Cochran Negro High School. Library established October 19, 1957.
Place	Cochran; Bleckley County GA.
Donor(s)	General contributions.
Notes	Edward D. Curry, school principal.

## and Name	93-
School	Millville Elementary/High School. Library established Nov. 23, 1957.
Place	Dudley; Laurens County GA.
Donor(s)	General contributions.
Notes	U.S. Toler, school principal.

## and Name	94-
School	Glenwood Consolidated School; Glenwood Elementary/High School. Library established December 18, 1957.
Place	Winder; Barrow County GA.
Donor(s)	General contributions.
Notes	L.D. Simon, school principal.

## and Name	95-
School	Calhoun Elementary/High School. Library established May 10, 1958.
Place	Irwinton; Wilkinson County GA.
Donor(s)	General contributions.
Notes	Robert C. Carruthers, school principal.

## and Name	96-
School	Earl Baker High School. Library established May 24, 1958.
Place	Newton; Baker County GA.
Donor(s)	General contributions.
Notes	E. James Grant, school principal.

## and Name	97-
School	Macon County Training School. Library established June 4, 1958.
Place	Montezuma; Macon County GA.
Donor(s)	General contributions.
Notes	William Newsom, school principal.

## and Name	98-
School	Peter G. Appling High School. Library established September 27, 1958.
Place	East Macon; Bibb County GA.
Donor(s)	General contributions.
Notes	Harry B. Thompson, school principal.

## and Name	99-
School	Jones County Training School; Maggie Califf Consolidated School. Library established September 27, 1958.
Place	Gray; Jones County GA.
Donor(s)	General contributions.
Notes	B.F. Crawford, school principal.

## and Name	100-
School	Burgess-Landrum High School. Library established November 5, 1958.
Place	Millen; Jenkins County GA.
Donor(s)	General contributions.
Notes	James L. Brown, school principal.

## and Name	101-
School	Southside Elementary/High School. Library established March 24, 1960.
Place	Colbert; Madison County GA.
Donor(s)	General contributions.
Notes	Mrs. Bertha Carithers, school principal.

## and Name	102-
School	Wilcox County Consolidated School. Library established June 14, 1960.
Place	Rochelle; Wilcox County GA.
Donor(s)	General contributions.
Notes	Eddie Daniel, school principal.

## and Name	103-
School	Sol C. Johnson High School. Library established 1960.
Place	Thunderbolt; Chatham County GA.
Donor(s)	General contributions.
Notes	Alflorence Cheatham, school principal.

## and Name	104-
School	Ed Stroud Elementary/High School. Library established 1960.
Place	Watkinsville; Oconee County GA.
Donor(s)	General contributions.
Notes	Theodore C. Dyson, school principal.

## and Name	105-
School	Warren County Training School. Library established March 20, 1961.
Place	Warrenton; Warren County GA.
Donor(s)	General contributions.
Notes	Mildred Freeman, school principal. Freeman Elementary School remains.

## and Name	106-
School	Tompkins High School. Library established March 25, 1961.
Place	Savannah; Chatham County GA.
Donor(s)	General contributions.
Notes	James Lutera, school principal; Mrs. A.B. Ingersoll, librarian.

## and Name	107-
School	Library established 1963.
Place	Leesburg; Lee County GA.
Donor(s)	General contributions.
Notes	

## and Name	108-
School	Library established 1963.
Place	Lexsy: Emanuel County GA.
Donor(s)	General contributions.
Notes	

## and Name	109-
School	A.C. Carter Elementary/High School. Library established December 13, 1965.
Place	Summerville; Chattooga County GA.
Donor(s)	General contributions. 3000 volumes.
Notes	J.L. Thomas, school principal.

## and Name	110-
School	Anderson Elementary School. Library established February 5, 1966.
Place	Leary; Calhoun County GA.
Donor(s)	General contributions. 3000 volumes.
Notes	J. Fred Oliver, school principal; Robert W. Green, librarian.

## and Name	111-
School	Miles College (sponsored by Christian Methodist Episcopal Church).
Place	Fairfield; Jefferson County AL.
Donor(s)	General contributions. 500 volumes given to college library.
Notes	Only donation recorded outside SC and GA.

## and Name	112-
School	Magnolia Grammar School.
Place	Valdosta; Lowndes County GA.
Donor(s)	General contributions; 2400 volumes.
Notes	L.E. Bell, school principal.

## and Name	113-
School	Vienna High/Industrial School.
Place	Vienna; Dooley County GA.
Donor(s)	General contributions.
Notes	Napoleon Williams, school principal.

## and Name	114-
School	Jefferson Negro School; Bryan High School.
Place	Jefferson; Jackson County GA.
Donor(s)	General contributions.
Notes	L.W. Jay, school principal.

## and Name	115-
School	Hunt High School.
Place	Fort Valley; Peach County GA.
Donor(s)	General contributions.
Notes	H.E. Bryant, school principal.

## and Name	116-
School	Fairmont High School.
Place	Griffin; Spalding County GA.
Donor(s)	General contributions.
Notes	C.W. Daniels, principal.

## and Name	117-
School	Royal Library.
Place	Cedartown; Polk County GA.
Donor(s)	General contributions.
Notes	

## and Name	118-
School	Treutlen County Training School.
Place	Soperton; Treutlen County GA.
Donor(s)	General contributions.
Notes	Augustus McArthur, principal.

## and Name	119-
School	Henry Tucker Singleton High School.
Place	Morgan; Calhoun County GA.
Donor(s)	General contributions.
Notes	James A. Slaton, school principal.

## and Name	120-
School	Carnesville Trade School.
Place	Carnesville; Franklin County GA.
Donor(s)	General contributions.
Notes	L.H. Hardy, Jr., school principal.

Bibliography

Allen, Francis W. "Faith Cabin Libraries.", *Library Journal* 66 (March 1, 1941), pp. 187-188.

"The Alumni Beat," *Chicago Defender* (October 30, 1965).

Announcements for 1942-1943. *The Benedict Bulletin*, Vol. 18, No.9. Benedict College, Columbia SC. Courtesy of Benedict College.

Announcements for 1943-1944. *The Benedict Bulletin*, Vol. 19, No.4. Benedict College, Columbia SC. Courtesy of Benedict College.

Announcements for 1944-1945. *The Benedict Bulletin*, Vol. 20, No.4. Benedict College, Columbia SC. Courtesy of Benedict College.

Another Special Life In Christ. Internet.http://poptop.hypermart.net/testwlb.html April 4, 2005.

"Augusta minister cited for establishing libraries," *Augusta (GA) Chronicle* (November 14, 1958).

"Augustan, Founder of Library Chain for Negroes, Receives $1,000 Award," *Augusta (GA) Herald* (November 13, 1958).

"Augustan will receive $1,000 service award," *Augusta (GA) Chronicle* (November 12, 1958).

Ausband, Jerry. "Faith Cabin Libraries Bring Books To Those Who Have None," *The Greenville (SC) News* (July 30, 1961).

Batten, Barton, Durstine & Osborne, Inc. Letter To Willie Lee Buffington; February 28, 1951.Courtesy of the South Caroliniana Library, University of South Carolina, Columbia SC.

Beard, Frederica. "A Mill Worker and His Dreams," *The Religious Telescope* (August 26, 1933). Courtesy of the South Caroliniana Library, University of South Carolina, Columbia SC.

Bennett, Louise, Brooks GA County Chamber of Commerce. Letter to Willie Lee Buffington; January 31, 1950. Courtesy of the South Caroliniana Library, University of South Carolina, Columbia SC.

_____ Letter to Willie Lee Buffington; January 31, 1950. Courtesy of the South Caroliniana Library, University of South Carolina, Columbia SC.

_____ Letter to Dr. Forrest C. Weir; May 22, 1950. Courtesy of the South Caroliniana Library, University of South Carolina, Columbia SC.

"Black Women's Oral History Project Interview with Virginia Lacy Jones," *The Georgia Librarian* 28 (Fall, 1991), pp. 82-85.

Blackburn, Dorothy R. Letter to Good Will Committee Members; undated. Courtesy of the South Caroliniana Library, University of South Carolina, Columbia SC.

Blair, Nancy. *Statewide Library Project Annual Report July1, 1939 – June 30, 1940*, pp.9-12, 22. Courtesy of the South Caroliniana Library, University of South Carolina, Columbia SC.

Brown, Earl R., Executive Secretary, Board of Missions and Church Extension of the Methodist Church. Letter to Willie Lee Buffington; December 14, 1948. Courtesy of the South Caroliniana Library, University of South Carolina, Columbia SC.

_____ Letter to Willie Lee Buffington; December 22, 1948. Courtesy of the South Caroliniana Library, University of South Carolina, Columbia SC.

Brown, Rev. George A. "By Faith Willie Lee Buffington," *The United Presbyterian* (December 30, 1937). Courtesy of the South Caroliniana Library, University of South Carolina, Columbia SC.

Buell, Earnest H. "Establishing Libraries As Community Centers In The Colored School Sections Of The South." Sociology Term Paper, Connecticut State College, 1937. Courtesy of Dan Lee, Presbyterian College.

Buffington, Willie L. *A Boy, A Dime, And A Miracle* (Part I); undated. Una R. Lawrence Papers, Southern Baptist Historical Library and Archives, Nashville TN.

_____ *A Boy, A Dime, And A Miracle* (Part II); undated. Una R. Lawrence Papers, Southern Baptist Historical Library and Archives, Nashville TN.

_____ Faith Cabin Library Needs Your Help; undated. Courtesy of the South Caroliniana Library, University of South Carolina, Columbia SC.

_____ *A General Survey of Faith Cabin Library With Its 26 Separate Units (South Carolina)*; June & July, 1940. Courtesy of the South Caroliniana Library, University of South Carolina, Columbia SC.

_____ Greetings to Faith Cabin Library Friends; June 1, 1955. Courtesy of the South Caroliniana Library, University of South Carolina, Columbia SC.

_____ High School Transcript. Registrar's Office, Berry College, Mt. Berry GA. Courtesy of Berry College Archives, Rome GA.

_____ How "Faith Cabin" Came Into Existence. Undated. Robert Burns Eleazer Papers, Vanderbilt University Special Collections.

_____ "How You Can Help Build A Library," *Comprehensive Guide for Bible Teaching*, (October-December, 1952). Published by David C. Cook, Publisher. Permission required to republish.

_____ "I Had Ten Cents – and a Dream," *Who* (February, 1942), pp.45-49. Courtesy of the South Caroliniana Library, University of South Carolina, Columbia SC.

_____ Interview, Saluda County Historical Society; May 6, 1987. Courtesy of Mary Parkman, Saluda SC.

_____ Letter to Dr. Will Alexander, Commission on Interracial Cooperation; February 15, 1933. Robert Burns Eleazer Papers, Vanderbilt University Special Collections.

_____Letter to Dr. Will Alexander, Commission on Interracial Cooperation; February 19, 1933. Robert Burns Eleazer Papers, Vanderbilt University Special Collections.

_____Letter to Dr. Will Alexander, Commission on Interracial Cooperation; March 3, 1933. Robert Burns Eleazer Papers, Vanderbilt University Special Collections.

_____Letter to Dr. Will Alexander, Commission on Interracial Cooperation; April 10, 1933. Robert Burns Eleazer Papers, Vanderbilt University Special Collections.

_____ Letter to Willie Buffington Jr., undated. Courtesy of the South Caroliniana Library, University of South Carolina, Columbia SC.

_____ Letter to Mrs. L.T. Clark, Southern Illinois Conference of Women's' Society of Christian Service; March 2, 1949. Courtesy of the South Caroliniana Library, University of South Carolina, Columbia SC.

_____Letter to Robert Cousins, Georgia State Department of Education; May 8, 1950. Courtesy of the South Caroliniana Library, University of South Carolina, Columbia SC.

_____Letter to Robert Cousins, Georgia State Department of Education; May11, 1950. Courtesy of the South Caroliniana Library, University of South Carolina, Columbia SC.

_____ Letter to "Dear Faith Cabin Library Friend"; October 2, 1942. Courtesy of the South Caroliniana Library, University of South Carolina, Columbia SC.

_____ Letter to "Faith Cabin Library Friends and Donors; November 6, 1933. Courtesy of the South Caroliniana Library, University of South Carolina, Columbia SC.

_____Letter to Dr. J.M. Ellison, President, Virginia Union University; May 11, 1950. Courtesy of the South Caroliniana Library, University of South Carolina, Columbia SC.

_____Letter to Mendel Fletcher, Registrar, Furman University; August 10, 1938. Courtesy of Furman University, Alumni Archives, Greenville SC.

_____Letter to Friends of Faith Cabin Library; March 1, 1960. Courtesy of the South Caroliniana Library, University of South Carolina, Columbia SC.

_____Letter to Dr. B.E. Geer, President Emeritus, Furman University; November 9, 1955. Courtesy of the South Caroliniana Library, University of South Carolina, Columbia SC.

149

_____ Letter to Genesee NY Conference of Women's Society of Christian Service; November 10, 1948. Courtesy of the South Caroliniana Library, University of South Carolina, Columbia SC.

_____ Letter to Rev. A.L. Gilmore, Christian Methodist Episcopal Church; May 11, 1950. Courtesy of the South Caroliniana Library, University of South Carolina, Columbia SC.

_____ Letter to E.F. Huff, Department of Education, White County GA; May 15, 1947. Courtesy of the South Caroliniana Library, University of South Carolina, Columbia SC.

_____ Letter to Mrs. David Jones, Bennett College; May 11, 1950. Courtesy of the South Caroliniana Library, University of South Carolina, Columbia SC.

_____ Letter to Roman Koral, Warsaw Poland; January 6, 1938. Courtesy of the South Caroliniana Library, University of South Carolina, Columbia SC.

_____ Letter to Miss Una R. Lawrence, Home Mission Board; August 4, 1944. Una R. Lawrence Papers, Southern Baptist Historical Library and Archives, Nashville TN.

_____ Letter to Miss Una R. Lawrence, Home Mission Board; August 20, 1944. Una R. Lawrence Papers, Southern Baptist Historical Library and Archives, Nashville TN.

_____ Letter to Miss Una R. Lawrence, Home Mission Board; January 9, 1946. Una R. Lawrence Papers, Southern Baptist Historical Library and Archives, Nashville TN.

_____ Letter fragment (likely to Miss Una R. Lawrence), untitled and undated. Una R. Lawrence Papers, Southern Baptist Historical Library and Archives, Nashville TN.

_____ Letter to Dr. Robert Lester, Executive Director, The Southern Fellowships Fund; September 30, 1956. Courtesy of the South Caroliniana Library, University of South Carolina, Columbia SC.

_____ Letter to local presidents of the Southern Illinois Conference of Women's Society of Christian Service; March 24, 1949. Courtesy of the South Caroliniana Library, University of South Carolina, Columbia SC.

_____Letter fragment to Dr. Edgar Love, Division of the Board of Missions and Church Extension of the Methodist Church; November 13, 1950. Courtesy of the South Caroliniana Library, University of South Carolina, Columbia SC.

_____Letter to Dr. Edward G. Mackey; May 11, 1950. Courtesy of the South Caroliniana Library, University of South Carolina, Columbia SC.

_____ Letter fragment (likely to Ted Malone), untitled and undated. Courtesy of the South Caroliniana Library, University of South Carolina, Columbia SC.

_____Letter to Mrs. Benjamin E. Mayes, Secretary, Faith Cabin Library Committee ; May 28, 1951. Courtesy of the South Caroliniana Library, University of South Carolina, Columbia SC.

_____Letter to Bishop Arthur Moore, President, Methodist Council of Bishops; February 18, 1949. Courtesy of the South Caroliniana Library, University of South Carolina, Columbia SC.

_____Letter to Bishop Arthur Moore, President, Methodist Council of Bishops; May 11, 1950. Courtesy of the South Caroliniana Library, University of South Carolina, Columbia SC.

_____Letter to Miss Nelle Morton, General Secretary of the Fellowship of Christian Churchmen; May 11, 1950. Courtesy of the South Caroliniana Library, University of South Carolina, Columbia SC.

_____Letter to NAACP; February 1, 1932. Special Collections and University Archives, W.E.B. DuBois Library, University of Massachusetts, Amherst MA.

_____Letter to Dr. George Nace, Executive Secretary, Home Missions Council of North America; April 29, 1950. Courtesy of the South Caroliniana Library, University of South Carolina, Columbia SC.

_____Letter to Mrs. Allen Newkirk, Southern Illinois Conference of Womens' Society of Christian Service; February 23, 1949. Courtesy of the South Caroliniana Library, University of South Carolina, Columbia SC.

_____Letter to the New York Conference of Womens' Society of Christian Service; October 1, 1947. Courtesy of the South Caroliniana Library, University of South Carolina, Columbia SC.

_____Letter to North Indiana Conference of Womens' Society of Christian Service; April 8, 1949. Courtesy of the South Caroliniana Library, University of South Carolina, Columbia SC.

_____Letter to Dr. F.D. Patterson, President of Tuskegee Institute; May 17, 1950. Courtesy of the South Caroliniana Library, University of South Carolina, Columbia SC.

_____Letter to Dr. E.C. Peters, President, Paine College; April 13, 1949. Courtesy of the South Caroliniana Library, University of South Carolina, Columbia SC.

_____Letter to Dr. Don Pielstick, Home Missions Council of North America, Inc; May 8, 1950. Courtesy of the South Caroliniana Library, University of South Carolina, Columbia SC.

_____Letter to Dr. Don Pielstick,Home Missions Council of North America, Inc; November 13, 1950. Courtesy of the South Caroliniana Library, University of South Carolina, Columbia SC.

_____Letter to Archie Polsky, The Polsky Foundation; May 19, 1950. Courtesy of the South Caroliniana Library, University of South Carolina, Columbia SC.

_____Letter to Dr. W.F. Quillian, President of Wesleyan College; May 11, 1950. Courtesy of the South Caroliniana Library, University of South Carolina, Columbia SC.

_____Letter to Dr. Harry V. Richardson, President of Gammon Theological Seminary; May 12, 1950. Courtesy of the South Caroliniana Library, University of South Carolina, Columbia SC.

_____Letter to Gwendolyn Ross; January 13, 1975. Courtesy of the South Caroliniana Library, University of South Carolina, Columbia SC.

_____Letter to Gwendolyn Ross; October 15, 1975. Courtesy of the South Caroliniana Library, University of South Carolina, Columbia SC.

_____ Letter to Dr. James Sells, Southeastern Office of the Methodist Church; May 7, 1950. Courtesy of the South Caroliniana Library, University of South Carolina, Columbia SC.

_____Letter to Dr. James Sells, Southeastern Office of the Methodist Church; May 17, 1950. Courtesy of the South Caroliniana Library, University of South Carolina, Columbia SC.

_____Letter to Thelma Stevens, Woman's Division of the Board of Missions and Church Extension of the Methodist Church; November 13, 1950. Courtesy of the South Caroliniana Library, University of South Carolina, Columbia SC.

_____Letter to Dr. Channing Tobias, Phelps-Stokes Fund; April 26, 1950. Courtesy of the South Caroliniana Library, University of South Carolina, Columbia SC.

_____Letter to Dr. Channing Tobias, Phelps-Stokes Fund; May 6, 1950. Courtesy of the South Caroliniana Library, University of South Carolina, Columbia SC.

_____Letter to Dr. Channing Tobias, Phelps-Stokes Fund; November 13, 1950. Courtesy of the South Caroliniana Library, University of South Carolina, Columbia SC.

_____Letter to W.D. Tolbert, Principal, Bryant Street School, Conyers GA; February 25, 1949. Courtesy of the South Caroliniana Library, University of South Carolina, Columbia SC.

_____Letter to Estellene Walker, Executive Secretary, SC State Library Board; December 18, 1947. Courtesy of the South Caroliniana Library, University of South Carolina, Columbia SC.

_____Letter to Dr. Forest W. Weir, Southeastern Inter-Council office of Home Missions Council of North America, Inc.; May 17, 1950. Courtesy of the South Caroliniana Library, University of South Carolina, Columbia SC.

_____ Memo: Containing Background Information Concerning An Appeal To Home Missions Council of North America To Sponsor and Support Faith Cabin Library Movement; November 13, 1950. Courtesy of the South Caroliniana Library, University of South Carolina, Columbia SC.

_____ "The Ministry of Books," *World Outlook: General Board of Global Ministries* (January 1955). Courtesy of the South Caroliniana Library, University of South Carolina, Columbia SC.

_____ "Saluda, S.C.," Community Organization Term Paper, Furman University, 1936.Courtesy of the South Caroliniana Library, University of South Carolina, Columbia SC.

_____ Script Describing The Kodachrome Slides Of the Faith Cabin Library. Undated. Courtesy of the South Caroliniana Library, University of South Carolina, Columbia SC.

_____ Sermon at Tignall United Methodist Church, Tignall GA, March 24, 1971. Courtesy of the South Caroliniana Library, University of South Carolina, Columbia SC.

_____ *Share A Book Today And Build Character For Tomorrow!* ; October 2, 1942. Courtesy of the South Caroliniana Library, University of South Carolina, Columbia SC.

_____ *The Story Of My Life*; undated.Robert Burns Eleazer Papers, Vanderbilt University Special Collections.

_____ *Suggestions For Collecting, And Instructions For Sending Books To Faith Cabin Library*; undated instructional sheet.

_____ "What A Dime and Faith Can Do," pp. 217-221; from Stefferud, Alfred (ed)., *The Wonderful World of Books*; New York: Mentor Books of The New American Library, 1952.

Burleigh, Betty. "Libraries in Cabins," *World Outlook: General Board of Global Ministries_* (March, 1946), pp. 5-8. Courtesy of the South Caroliniana Library, University of South Carolina, Columbia SC.

Caldwell, I.S. "Bread Cast Upon The Waters Is Returning", (undated pamphlet). Courtesy of the South Caroliniana Library, University of South Carolina, Columbia SC.

_____ "Truth Is Stanger Than Fiction," *Augusta (GA) Herald* (October, 1933). Courtesy of the South Caroliniana Library, University of South Carolina, Columbia SC. Courtesy of the *Augusta (GA) Herald.*

Calhoun, E. Clayton, President, Paine College. Letter to Willie Lee Buffington; July 2, 1956. Courtesy of the South Caroliniana Library, University of South Carolina, Columbia SC. Courtesy of Paine College Library.

_____ Letter to Willie Lee Buffington; April 5, 1967. Courtesy of the South Caroliniana Library, University of South Carolina, Columbia SC. Courtesy of Paine College Library.

_____ Letter to Willie Lee Buffington; April 15, 1967. Courtesy of the South Caroliniana Library, University of South Carolina, Columbia SC. Courtesy of Paine College Library.

Cameron, Erma and Daniel T. Grant, Washington Consolidated Schools, Cairo GA. Letter to Willie Lee Buffington; March 11, 1957. Courtesy of the South Caroliniana Library, University of South Carolina, Columbia SC.

Carr, Louise D. "The Reverend Willie Lee Buffington's Life and Contributions To The Development Of Rural Libraries In The South." Master's Thesis, Atlanta University, 1958. Courtesy of Archives Research Center, Robert W. Woodruff Library, Atlanta University, Atlanta GA.

_____ Letter to Willie Lee Buffington; August 3, 1957. Courtesy of the South Caroliniana Library, University of South Carolina, Columbia SC.

Carter, Paul C. and Ruth H. Geil. "Faith Cabin Libraries", *Baptist Leader* (November, 1943). Courtesy of the South Caroliniana Library, University of South Carolina, Columbia SC.

Cherry, Dr. Maurice, Retired Chaplain, Paine College. Telephone interview; January 6, 2011.

Clarke, M.A., Carver High School, Douglas GA. Letter to Willie Lee Buffington; March 16, 1949. Courtesy of the South Caroliniana Library, University of South Carolina, Columbia SC.

Clayton, Dr. Marcus. Retired Professor, Paine College. Telephone interview; January 2, 2011.

Columbia (SC) State (May 1, 1933). Courtesy of the South Caroliniana Library, University of South Carolina, Columbia SC. Courtesy of The Columbia *State*, Columbia SC.

Cousins, Robert L., Georgia State Department of Education. Letter to Frary Elrod, Superintendent, Jackson County GA Schools; October 10, 1957. Courtesy of the South Caroliniana Library, University of South Carolina, Columbia SC.

155

_____ Letter to D.F. Osborne, Superintendent, Winder City GA Schools; November 14, 1957.Courtesy of the South Caroliniana Library, University of South Carolina, Columbia SC.

_____ Letter to Dr. Forrest Weir, Southeastern Inter-Council Office; May 22, 1950. Courtesy of the South Caroliniana Library, University of South Carolina, Columbia SC.

Crozer Theological Seminary Alumni Association File on Willie Lee Buffington.

Cummings, Robert. Letter to Willie Lee Buffington; April 17, 1951. Courtesy of the South Caroliniana Library, University of South Carolina, Columbia SC.

Curtis, Anna L. "Libraries By Faith," *Classmates* (July, 1942).

Davis, Bert H. "Feeding The Book-Hungry," *The Christian Advocate* (July 24, 1941).

Daytona Beach (FL) Morning Journal (April 11, 1964).

Dedicatory Program of the Faith Cabin Library, Brooks High School, Quitman GA (May 14, 1950). Courtesy of the South Caroliniana Library, University of South Carolina, Columbia SC.

Degen, Catherine. Letter to Willie Lee Buffington; February, 19, 1938. Courtesy of the South Caroliniana Library, University of South Carolina, Columbia SC.

A Dime's Worth of Books: A Program That Brought Books to Southern Negro Communities. Charlottesville, VA, University of Virginia: Extension Division Bulletin, New Dominion Series, #130; January, 1952.

Dowell, Kathy Henry. "Student Intern Discovers The Willie Lee Buffington Collection," *University South Caroliniana Society Newsletter* (Fall, 2011), p.3.

"Dr. Lucius Pitts," *Augusta (GA) Chronicle* (March 27, 1974).

Eaton, Ethel M. "Coming in on a Dime and a Prayer," *The Saturday Evening Post* (November 27, 1943), p. 18.

_____ "28 Libraries Started on Dime and Prayer," *The Afro American* (January29, 1944), p.2.

Eatonton Colored High School Dedicatorial Service For Faith Cabin Library; October 7, 1949. Courtesy of the South Caroliniana Library, University of South Carolina, Columbia SC.

"Edgefield Cotton Mill Boy Establishes Libraries For Colored People Of Section," *Greenville(SC) News* (April 28, 1935).

Elyria (OH) *Chronicle-Telegram* (September 15, 1939), p.1. Courtesy of the South Caroliniana Library, University of South Carolina, Columbia SC. Courtesy of Elyria *Chronicle-Telegram*, Elyria OH.

"Elyrians Make Libraries Possible," The Elyria (OH) *Chronicle-Telegram* (September 1, 1938), p.1. Courtesy of the South Caroliniana Library, University of South Carolina, Columbia SC. Courtesy of Elyria *Chronicle-Telegram*, Elyria OH.

Embree, Edwin R. and Julia Waxman. *Investment In People: The Story of the Julius Rosenwald Fund*. New York: Harper & Brothers Publishers, 1949.

"Enough Books For Two Libraries Given By Elyrians," *The Elyria (OH) Chronicle-Telegram* (November 12, 1938), p.2.Courtesy of the South Caroliniana Library, University of South Carolina, Columbia SC. Courtesy of Elyria *Chronicle-Telegram*, Elyria OH.

"Faculty Member at Paine College wins scholarship," *Augusta (GA) Chronicle* (April 12, 1956).

"The Faith Cabin Libraries," *Christian Index File* (March 1, 1956), Special Collections, Collins-Callaway Library, Paine College. Courtesy of Paine College Library, Augusta GA.

"Faith Cabin Library," *Christian Index File* (July 12, 1956), Special Collections, Collins-Callaway Library, Paine College. Courtesy of Paine College Library, Augusta GA.

"Faith Cabin," *The Crisis* (March, 1933), p.63.

"Faith Cabin Library Built By W.L. Buffington," *The Saluda (SC) Standard* (June 8, 1933), p.1. Courtesy of the Saluda *Standard*, Saluda SC.

"Faith Cabin Library To Open Monday," *The Clinch County (GA) News*, December 29, 1950.

"Fellowship Given Paine Professor," *Augusta (GA) Herald* (May 2, 1968).

157

Fenstermaker, Suzy. "Libraries Built By Faith," *Prism* (1984).

Forbush, Bliss. "Faith Cabin Libraries," *Friends Journal*, No.15, vol.7 (August 1, 1961), pp. 314-315.

"Founded 98 Libraries, Professor Gets $1000 Award," *Jet Magazine* (November 27, 1958), p.24.

Fulmer, Henry G. "The Faith Cabin Libraries Collection: New Materials, New Insights." University of South Carolina: University of South Carolina Libraries – *Caroliniana Columns*, Issue 17, Spring 2005, pp 1-2.

"Furman Student Starts Movement for Establishment of Negro Libraries," *The Greenville (SC)News* (April 26, 1936), p.4.

Furman University Alumni Association File on Willie Lee Buffington.

Geer, Dr. B.E., President Emeritus Furman University. Letter To Willie Lee Buffington; March 14, 1951. Courtesy of the South Caroliniana Library, University of South Carolina, Columbia SC.

Gomillion, C.G. Dean of Students, Tuskegee Institute. Letter to Willie Lee Buffington; April 9, 1957. Courtesy of the South Caroliniana Library, University of South Carolina, Columbia SC.

Gorman, Robert M. "Blazing The Way: The WPA Library Service Demonstration Project in South Carolina," *Library and Culture Journal 32 (4)* (Fall, 1997), pp. 427-455.

"Grant WSCS to Collect Magazines and Books for Children," *Cass City (MI) Chronicle* (February 3, 1950), p.8.

Gray, Emma C.W. "Buffington's Dream," Adult Student, (March, 1955). Published by David C. Cook , Publisher. Publisher permission required to reproduce.

_____ "A Man and His Ministry of Books," *Comprehensive Guide for Bible Study*, (October-December, 1952). Published by David C. Cook , Publisher. Publisher permission required to reproduce.

Henderson, A. Scott. "Building Intelligent And Active Public Minds: Education And Social Reform in Greenville County During the 1930s," *The South Carolina HistoricalMagazine*, Vol.106, No.1 (January, 2005), pp. 34-58.

Hightower, James R., Principal, Thomaston GA Training School. Letter to Willie Lee Buffington; November 3, 1949. Courtesy of the South Caroliniana Library, University of South Carolina, Columbia SC.

Hobert, Benjamin F. "Negroes Succeed In Georgia," Savannah (GA) *Morning News* (November 9, 1948). Courtesy of the Savannah Morning News, Savannah GA.

Holleman, Joey. "Segregation spurred S.C. School building spree," *The Columbia (SC) State*, February 9, 2010.

Holt, Dr. Arthur. Interview; June 11, 2010.

_____ E-mail Interview April 26, 2010.

_____ E-mail interview September 7, 2012.

_____ *The 5K Buffet*, Sermon at Memorial United Methodist Church (August 3, 2008).

_____ Unpublished pamphlet, 1989.

The Hornet: Furman University Magazine (January 31, 1936), pp. 1, 5.

Huff, E.J. Letter from Department of Education, White County GA, To Willie Lee Buffington; May 12, 1947. Courtesy of the South Caroliniana Library, University of South Carolina, Columbia SC.

Inman, Dave. *Hobby Lobby Radio Script*; undated. Courtesy of the South Caroliniana Library, University of South Carolina, Columbia SC.

Johnson, Charles Spurgeon. *Into The Mainstream:A Survey of Best Practices in Race Relations in the South* (e-book).

Jones, Karen M. "The Proper Setting for a Miracle," *Advance* (May 1937).Courtesy of the South Caroliniana Library, University of South Carolina, Columbia SC.

Jones, Virginia Lacy. "A Genuine Effort to Seek Truth," *Library Journal*, 88, No.22 (December 15, 1963), pp. 4703-4705. Courtesy of the *Library Journal*, New York, NY.

King, A.H, Associate Dean, University of NC. Letter to Willie Lee Buffington.; May 2, 1956. Courtesy of the South Caroliniana Library, University of South Carolina, Columbia SC.

Koral, Roman. Letter to Willie Lee Buffington; January 12, 1937. Courtesy of the South Caroliniana Library, University of South Carolina, Columbia SC.

Kuyper, George. "An Adventure In Faith," *Southern Workman* (May, 1933). Courtesy of Hampton University Archives. Courtesy of the South Caroliniana Library, University of South Carolina, Columbia SC.

Lane Bryant Annual Awards Ceremony Program (1958). Courtesy of Paine College Library, Augusta GA.

Lawrence, Una R., Home Mission Board. Letter to Willie Lee Buffington; August 12, 1944. Una R. Lawrence Papers, Southern Baptist Historical Library and Archives, Nashville TN.

_____ Letter fragment to Willie Lee Buffington; undated. Una R. Lawrence Papers, Southern Baptist Historical Library and Archives, Nashville TN.

Lee, Dan. "From Segregation to Integration: Library Services for Blacks in South Carolina, 1923 – 1962." From John M. Tucker (ed.) *Untold Stories: Civil Rights, Libraries and Black Librarianship.* Champaign IL: University of Illinois Graduate School of Library and Information Services, 1998. Courtesy of the author.

_____ "Faith Cabin Libraries: A Study of an Alternative Library Service in the Segregated South, 1932-1960," *Library History Seminar* VIII (May, 1990), pp 170-182. Courtesy of the author.

Let There Be Light; undated pamphlet. Courtesy of the South Caroliniana Library, University of South Carolina, Columbia SC.

"Library for Negro School Result Of One Young White Man's Interest," Saluda (SC) *Standard* (May 9, 1933). Courtesy of the Saluda *Standard*, Saluda SC.

"Library Founder In Backwoods To Speak Here Friday." Xenia (OH) *Evening Gazette*, August 5, 1936, p.8. Courtesy of Xenia *Daily Gazette*, Xenia OH.

"Makes Final Appeal To Elyrians For Faith Cabin Library," Elyria (OH) *Chronicle-Telegram* (July 23, 1938), p.2. Courtesy of Elyria *Chronicle-Telegram*, Elyria OH.

Malone, Ted. *Westinghouse Presents*, Broadcast Script (October 6, 1948). Courtesy of the South Caroliniana Library, University of South Carolina, Columbia SC.

Maynard, Edwin. "New Hope From Old Books," *The Kiwanis Magazine* (February 1950).

"Meeting Held By Faith Cabin Library Committee." Iowa City (IA) *Press-Citizen*, February 20, 1937. Courtesy of Iowa City *Press-Citizen*, Iowa City IA.

Middleton, W. Vernon, Division of National Missions of the Board of Missions of the Methodist Church. Letter to Willie Lee Buffington; March 28, 1956. Courtesy of the South Caroliniana Library, University of South Carolina, Columbia SC.

Millender, Mallory K. "Dr. Buffington Is News-Review's Citizen Of The Year," *Augusta (GA) News-Review*, Vol.5, #13 (June 19, 1975).Courtesy of the author.

Monk, John. White Man Struggled To Bring Books to Poor Blacks," *Columbia (SC) State*, April 4, 2005.

Mt. Berry School, Rome GA, High School Transcripts for Willie Lee Buffington, 1926-27. Courtesy of Mt. Berry School, Rome GA.

Murchison, Anna L. "He Builds Libraries for Negroes," *Southern Baptist Home Missions* (November, 1942). Una R. Lawrence Papers, Southern Baptist Historical Library and Archives, Nashville TN.

Murray, Carol. "Danville Woman Gives Away Books," *Danville (IL) Commercial News* (September 2, 1951).

Neal, Harry Edward. "The Bookshelves Filled by Faith," *David C. Cook Sunday Digest* (April 12, 1959). (*Sunday Digest* is published by David C. Cook). Publisher permission required to reproduce.

Norman, Jr., Dr. Silas. E-mail Interview January 26, 2011.

O'Donnell, Suzanna W. "Equal Opportunities For Both: Julius
    Rosenwald, Jim Crow, and the Charleston Free Library's Record Of
    Service To Blacks, 1931 To 1960." Master's Thesis, University of
    North Carolina, 2000. Courtesy of the author.

"175 lbs. of new and used books have been sent to Faith Cabin Library,"
    Emporia (KS) Gazette (February 12, 1962).

Paine College. *Annual Report, Faith Cabin Library Extension of Paine College:
    To the Board of Trustees.* 1950-51. Courtesy of Paine College Library,
    Augusta GA.

_____*Annual Report, Faith Cabin Library Extension of Paine
    College: To the Board of Trustees.* 1951-52. Courtesy of Paine College
    Library, Augusta GA.

_____*Annual Report, Faith Cabin Library Extension of Paine
    College: To the Board of Trustees.* 1952-53. Courtesy of Paine College
    Library, Augusta GA.

_____*Annual Report, Faith Cabin Library Extension of Paine
    College: To the Board of Trustees.* 1953-54. Courtesy of Paine College
    Library, Augusta GA.

_____*Annual Report, Faith Cabin Library Extension of Paine
    College: To the Board of Trustees.* 1956-57. Courtesy of Paine College
    Library, Augusta GA.

_____*Annual Report, Faith Cabin Library Extension of Paine
    College: To the Board of Trustees._* 1957-58. Courtesy of Paine College
    Library, Augusta GA.

_____*Board of Trustees Meeting Minutes.* May 24, 1951. Courtesy
    of Paine College Library, Augusta GA.

_____*Board of Trustees Meeting Minutes.* May 20, 1960. Courtesy
    of Paine College Library, Augusta GA.

_____*Board of Trustees Meeting Minutes.* April 1-2, 1963. Courtesy
    of Paine College Library, Augusta GA.

_____*Board of Trustees Meeting Minutes.* May 7-8, 1965. Courtesy
    of Paine College Library, Augusta GA.

_____*Board of Trustees Meeting Minutes.* February 10, 1967. Courtesy of Paine College Library, Augusta GA.

_____*Board of Trustees Meeting Minutes.* February 9-10, 1968. Courtesy of Paine College Library, Augusta GA.

_____*Board of Trustees Meeting Minutes.* April 26, 1969. Courtesy of Paine College Library, Augusta GA.

_____*Board of Trustees Meeting Minutes.* May 3, 1975. Courtesy of Paine College Library, Augusta GA.

_____*Committee on Faith Cabin Library Report to theBoard of Trustees.* May 25, 1951. Courtesy of Paine College Library, Augusta GA.

_____*Faith Cabin Library Extension of Paine College, Proposed   Budget July 1,1952 – June 30, 1953.* Courtesy of Paine College Library, Augusta GA.

_____*Faith Cabin Library Report to the Student-Faculty Assembly;* December 6, 1949. Courtesy of Paine College Library, Augusta GA.

_____*Faith Cabin Library Report to the Student-Faculty Assembly;* February 7, 1950. Courtesy of Paine College Library, Augusta GA.

_____*Faith Cabin Library Report to the Student-Faculty Assembly;* April 25, 1950. Courtesy of Paine College Library, Augusta GA.

_____*Faith Cabin Library Report to the Student-Faculty Assembly;* December 12, 1950. Courtesy of Paine College Library, Augusta GA.

_____*Faith Cabin Library Report to the Student-Faculty Assembly;* February 1, 1951. Courtesy of Paine College Library, Augusta GA.

_____*Faith Cabin Library Report to the Student-Faculty Assembly;* April 16, 1951. Courtesy of Paine College Library, Augusta GA.

_____*Faith Cabin Library Report to the Student-Faculty Assembly;* October 2, 1951. Courtesy of Paine College Library, Augusta GA.

_____*Faith Cabin Library Report to the Student-Faculty Assembly;* December 11, 1951. Courtesy of Paine College Library, Augusta GA.

163

_____*Faith Cabin Library Report to the Student-Faculty Assembly*; April 28, 1952. Courtesy of Paine College Library, Augusta GA.

_____*Faith Cabin Library Report to the Student-Faculty Assembly*; February 8, 1954. Courtesy of Paine College Library, Augusta GA.

_____Pre-College Reading Program, 1968-1969. Courtesy of Paine College Library, Augusta GA.

_____*President's Report to the Board of Trustees.* May 20, 1960. Courtesy of Paine College Library, Augusta GA.

_____*Report of Faith Cabin Library Extension of Paine College: To the Board of Trustees*; May 25, 1950. Courtesy of Paine College Library, Augusta GA.

_____*Report of Faith Cabin Library Extension of Paine College: To the Executive Committee of Board of Trustees*; October 4, 1951. Courtesy of Paine College Library, Augusta GA.

_____*Report of Faith Cabin Library Extension of Paine College: To the Executive Committee of Board of Trustees*; October 28, 1960. Courtesy of Paine College Library, Augusta GA.

_____*Report of Faith Cabin Library Extension of Paine College: To the Executive Committee of Board of Trustees*; December 9-10, 1965. Courtesy of Paine College Library, Augusta GA.

_____*Report of Faith Cabin Library Extension of Paine College: To the Executive Committee of Board of Trustees*; February 10, 1966. Courtesy of Paine College Library, Augusta GA.

_____*Report of Faith Cabin Library Extension of Paine College: To the Executive Committee of Board of Trustees*; April 25, 1970. Courtesy of Paine College Library, Augusta GA.

_____*Report of Faith Cabin Library Extension of Paine College: To the Executive Committee of Board of Trustees*; April 28-29, 1972. Courtesy of Paine College Library, Augusta GA.

_____*Report to the Board of Trustees.* May 21, 1948. Courtesy of Paine College Library, Augusta GA.

_____*Report to the Board of Trustees.* April, 1957. Courtesy of Paine College Library, Augusta GA.

_____*Report to the Board of Trustees.* May, 1958. Courtesy of Paine College Library, Augusta GA.

_____Salary Contract Between Paine College and Rev. W.L. Buffington, 1949-1950. Courtesy of Paine College Library, Augusta GA.

_____Salary Contract Between Paine College and Rev. W.L. Buffington, 1956-1957. Courtesy of Paine College Library, Augusta GA.

_____Salary Contract Between Paine College and Rev. W.L. Buffington, 1962-1963. Courtesy of Paine College Library, Augusta GA.

_____Salary Contract Between Paine College and Rev. W.L. Buffington, 1967-1968. Courtesy of Paine College Library, Augusta GA.

_____Salary Contract Between Paine College and Rev. W.L. Buffington, 1973-1974. Courtesy of Paine College Library, Augusta GA.

"Paine Minister Wins Public Service Award," *Augusta (GA) Herald* (November 11, 1958).

Parkman, Mary. Interview, April 11, 2010.

_____ "The Rev. Willie Lee Buffington", from *Our Saluda County Ancestors.* Vol.3, 2000, p.10.

"People With A Purpose," *Readers Digest* (January, 1937), p.97.

Peters, E.C. "Faith Cabin Libraries," *World Outlook: General Board of Global Ministries* (July, 1940), 10-11,31. Courtesy of the South Caroliniana Library, University of South Carolina, Columbia SC.

Pielstick, Don F., Home Missions Council of North America, Inc. Letter to Willie Lee Buffington; May 4, 1950. Courtesy of the South Caroliniana Library, University of South Carolina, Columbia SC.

Plumb, Beatrice. "The Brotherhood of Books," *Christian Herald* (July 1, 1933), pp. 16-18. Courtesy of the South Caroliniana Library, University of South Carolina, Columbia SC.

_____ "Joy Bells Ringing," *Christian Herald* (December, 1935). Courtesy of the South Caroliniana Library, University of South Carolina, Columbia SC.

_____ "A Dream, a Dime – and Faith," (pp.12-30) from *Lives That Inspire*. Minneapolis MN: T.S. Denison, 1962.

Polsky, Archie, The Polsky Foundation. Letter to Willie Lee Buffington; May 1, 1950. Courtesy of the South Caroliniana Library, University of South Carolina, Columbia SC.

Powell, Tamara S. "Communities In Collaboration: A Struggle To Increase Literacy In South Carolina." Master's Thesis, University of South Carolina, 2004. Used by permission of thesis advisor, Dr. Robert Williams.

Radford, Ruby. "Faith Cabin Library," *The Message Magazine* (May-June, 1960), pp. 24-25, 30.

Red Bank (NJ) Register (March 18, 1954).

"Rev. Buffington, retired minister and professor, dies," *The Greenville (SC) News*, April 7, 1988.

"The Rev. W.L. Buffington Sr., retired Methodist minister," *The Columbia (SC) State*, April 7, 1988.

Rosenwald School Legacy. http:sc.gov/rosenwaldschools.htm. (March 23, 2011).

SCMC 45-51. Willie Lee Buffington Home Movies. University of South Carolina.

Schramm-Pate, Susan and Rhonda B. Jeffries. *Grappling With Diversity: Readings on Civil Rights Pedagogy and Critical Multiculturalism*; Chapter 4, pp.75-95. Albany NY: State University of New York Press, 2008.

Sells, James W., Southeastern Office of the Methodist Church. Letter to Willie Lee Buffington; May 15, 1950. Courtesy of the South Caroliniana Library, University of South Carolina, Columbia SC.

"South Caroliniana Library Receives New Materials for Faith Cabin Libraries Collection," *Reflections* (Spring, 2004), p.5.

166

"Southern Story," *Florence (SC) Morning News* (January 23, 1951), p.4.

Sprinkle, Jr., Henry C. "The Miracle of the Books," *World Outlook: General Board of Global Ministries* (September, 1950). Courtesy of the South Caroliniana Library, University of South Carolina, Columbia SC.

Stanford, Edward Barrett. *Library Extension Under The Works Progress Administration (Chapter 6)*. Chicago: University of Chicago Press, 1941; pp.146, 152, 179, 180-185.

Stevens, Thelma, Woman's Division of the Board of Missions and Church Extension of the Methodist Church . Letter to Willie Lee Buffington; December 27, 1948. Courtesy of the South Caroliniana Library, University of South Carolina, Columbia SC.

Styler, Herman."Books for the Backwoods," *Together* (April 1961), pp.17-19.Courtesy of the South Caroliniana Library, University of South Carolina, Columbia SC.

_____ "He Worked Wonders –With Faith and a Dime," *Coronet* Vol.22, No.2 (June, 1947), pp.44-47. Courtesy of the South Caroliniana Library, University of South Carolina, Columbia SC.

"They Do Things Differently," *Readers Digest* (February, 1951).

"To Receive Alumni Achievement Award." *The Saluda (SC) Sentinel* (November 4, 1965).

Tobias, Dr. Channing. Letters Between Channing Tobias and Willie Lee Buffington (October 11,1932 – December 14, 1942). Kautz Family YMCA Archives, University of Minnesota Libraries.

_____ Letter from Phelps-Stokes Fund To Willie Lee Buffington; April 27, 1950. Kautz Family YMCA Archives, University of Minnesota Libraries.

University of Pennsylvania, University Archives and Records Center. Willie L. Buffington Biographical File.

Voils, Jessie Wiley, Assistant to Ted Malone, Westinghouse. Letter to Willie Lee Buffington; April 15, 1948. Courtesy of the South Caroliniana Library, University of South Carolina, Columbia SC.

Walker, Estellene, Executive Secretary, SC State Library Board. Letter to Willie Lee Buffington; November 15, 1947. Courtesy of the South Caroliniana Library, University of South Carolina, Columbia SC.

Watson, Reverend John. Letter to Willie Lee Buffington; October 13, 1933. Kautz Family YMCA Archives, University of Minnesota Libraries.

Weir, Dr. Forrest C, Southeastern Inter-Council Office, Home Missions Council of North America Inc. Letter to Willie Lee Buffington; May 19, 1950. Courtesy of the South Caroliniana Library, University of South Carolina, Columbia SC.

West, W.E., Principal, Jeffersonville GA. Letter to Willie Lee Buffington; March 28, 1949. Courtesy of the South Caroliniana Library, University of South Carolina, Columbia SC.

"W.L. Buffington Sr., retired minister, dies," *The Greenville (SC) Piedmont*, April 8, 1988.

Wishengrad, Morton. *Uncle Eury's Dollar*. The DuPont Company Presents The Cavalcade Of America, Broadcast Script (February 26, 1951). Courtesy of the South Caroliniana Library, University of South Carolina, Columbia SC.

Woodson, Hortense. "Mill Operative Founds Libraries Over State," *Spartanburg (SC) Herald-Journal*, May 4, 1935.

"A Worthwhile Cause," *The Richmond (VA) Times-Dispatch* (September 5, 1933), p., 6.

Yonkers (NY) Herald-Statesman (May 5, 1947).

Index

Chapter Notes

Chapter 1
[1] Willie Lee Buffington Interview, Saluda Historical Society (Saluda, 1987), 17-18.
[2]Ibid., 21.
[3]Ibid., 3.
[4] Willie Lee Buffington, Letter to Dr. Channing Tobias, October 11, 1932. Kautz Family YMCA Archives, University of Minnesota Libraries.
[5] Willie Lee Buffington, Letter to Una R. Lawrence, January 9, 1946. Una R. Lawrence Papers, Southern Baptist Historical Library and Archives, Nashville TN.
[6] Buffington Interview, 17.
[7]Ibid., 18-19.
[8] Harry Edward Neal, "The Bookshelves Filled By Faith," *David C. Cook Sunday Digest* (April 12, 1959). (Sunday Digest is published by David C. Cook). Publisher permission required to reproduce.
[9] Buffington Interview, 19.
[10] Willie Lee Buffington, *How Faith Cabin Came Into Existence* (undated). Robert Burns Eleazer Papers, Vanderbilt University Special Collections.
[11]Ibid.
[12] Ernest Buell, "Establishing Libraries As Community Centers In The Colored School Sections of The South" (Sociology Term Paper, Connecticut State College, 1937), p.6.
[13] Dr. Channing Tobias, Letter to Willie Lee Buffington, undated. Kautz Family YMCA Archives, University of Minnesota Libraries.
[14] Buffington Interview, 9.
[15]Ibid., 19-20.
[16]Ibid., 9.
[17] Buffington, *How Faith Cabin Came Into Existence* (undated). Robert Burns Eleazer Papers, Vanderbilt University Special Collections.
[18]Beatrice Plumb, "Joy Bells Ringing," *Christian Herald* (December, 1935), 1.Courtesy of the South Caroliniana Library, University of South Carolina, Columbia SC.

Chapter 2
[19]Frederica Beard, "A Mill Worker and His Dreams," *The Religious Telescope* (August 26, 1933), 1.Courtesy of the South Caroliniana Library, University of South Carolina, Columbia SC.
[20] Buell, pp. 6-7.

[21] Tamara S.Powell, "Communities In Collaboration: A Struggle To Increase Literacy In South Carolina" (Masters Thesis, University of South Carolina, 2004), p.77. Used by permission of thesis advisor, Dr. Robert Williams.
[22] Plumb, p.1.
[23] Beatrice Plumb, "A Dream, A Dime – and Faith", from *Lives That Inspire*.(T.S.Denison: Minneapolis MN, 1962), p.23.
[24] Buell, p.7.
[25] Plumb, *Lives That Inspire*, p.25.
[26] Buell, p.8.
[27] *The Saluda (SC) Standard*, June 8, 1933, p.1.
[28] Willie Lee Buffington, Letter to The National Association for the Advancement of Colored People, February 1, 1932. Special Collections and University Archives, W.E.B. DuBois Library, University of Massachusetts, Amherst MA.

Chapter 3
[29] I.S. Caldwell, "Truth Is Stranger Than Fiction," *Augusta (GA) Herald* (October, 1933).
[30] Beard, p.1.
[31] Buffington, Letter to Dr. Channing Tobias, October 11, 1932. Kautz Family YMCA Archives, University of Minnesota Libraries.
[32] Ibid.
[33] Ibid.
[34] Tobias, Letter to Willie Lee Buffington, November 5, 1932. Kautz Family YMCA Archives, University of Minnesota Libraries.
[35] Buffington, Letter to Dr. Channing Tobias, November 9, 1932. Kautz Family YMCA Archives, University of Minnesota Libraries.
[36] Ibid.
[37] Buffington, Letter to Dr. Channing Tobias, February 13, 1933. Kautz Family YMCA Archives, University of Minnesota Libraries.
[38] Ibid.
[39] Ibid.
[40] Ibid.
[41] Buffington, Letter to Dr. Channing Tobias, October 11, 1932. Kautz Family YMCA Archives, University of Minnesota Libraries.
[42] Buffington, Letter to Dr. Channing Tobias, November 9, 1932. Kautz Family YMCA Archives, University of Minnesota Libraries.
[43] Willie Lee Buffington, Letter to Dr. Channing Tobias, February 28, 1933. Kautz Family YMCA Archives, University of Minnesota Libraries.
[44] Ibid.
[45] Willie Lee Buffington, Letter to Dr. Will Alexander, February 15, 1933. Robert Burns Eleazer Papers, Vanderbilt University Special Collections.
[46] Willie Lee Buffington, Letter to Dr. Will Alexander, February 19, 1933. Robert Burns Eleazer Papers, Vanderbilt University Special Collections.

[47] Willie Lee Buffington, Letter to Dr. Will Alexander, March 3, 1933. Robert Burns Eleazer Papers, Vanderbilt University Special Collections.
[48] Willie Lee Buffington, Letter to Dr. Will Alexander, April, 1933. Robert Burns Eleazer Papers, Vanderbilt University Special Collections.
[49] Willie Lee Buffington, Letter to Dr. Channing Tobias, March 25, 1933. Kautz Family YMCA Archives, University of Minnesota Libraries.
[50] Ibid.
[51] Willie Lee Buffington, Letter to Dr. Channing Tobias, April 21, 1933. Kautz Family YMCA Archives, University of Minnesota Libraries.

Chapter 4
[52] Willie Lee Buffington, *The Story of My Life* (undated). Robert Burns Eleazer Papers, Vanderbilt University Special Collections.
[53] Willie Lee Buffington, Letter to Dr. Channing Tobias, January 29, 1933. Kautz Family YMCA Archives, University of Minnesota Libraries.
[54] Beatrice Plumb, "The Brotherhood of Books," *Christian Herald* (July 1, 1933), 18.Courtesy of the South Caroliniana Library, University of South Carolina, Columbia SC.
[55] Buffington, Letter to Dr. Channing Tobias, February 13, 1933. Kautz Family YMCA Archives, University of Minnesota Libraries.
[56] "Meeting Held By Faith Cabin Library Committee," *Iowa City (IA) Press-Citizen* (February 20, 1937).
[57] Willie Lee Buffington, *Faith Cabin Library Needs Your Help* (undated).
[58] Buffington, Letter to Dr. Channing Tobias, March 25, 1933. Kautz Family YMCA Archives, University of Minnesota Libraries.
[59] Ibid.
[60] Buffington, Letter to Dr. Channing Tobias, February 28, 1933. Kautz Family YMCA Archives, University of Minnesota Libraries.
[61] Buffington, Letter to Dr. Channing Tobias, April 21, 1933. Kautz Family YMCA Archives, University of Minnesota Libraries.
[62] Buffington, Letter to Dr. Channing Tobias, February 28, 1933. Kautz Family YMCA Archives, University of Minnesota Libraries.
[63] Buffington, Letter to Dr. Channing Tobias, March 25, 1933. Kautz Family YMCA Archives, University of Minnesota Libraries.
[64] Ibid.
[65] Buffington, Letter to Dr. Channing Tobias, April 21, 1933. Kautz Family YMCA Archives, University of Minnesota Archives.
[66] Ibid.
[67] Ibid.
[68] Ibid.
[69] *Columbia (SC) State*, May 1, 1933. Courtesy of the South Caroliniana Library, University of South Carolina, Columbia SC.
[70] Ibid.

[71] Willie Lee Buffington, Letter to Faith Cabin Library Friends and Donors, November 6, 1933. Kautz Family YMCA Archives, University of Minnesota Libraries.
[72] Ibid.
[73] Willie Lee Buffington, Letter to Gwendolyn Ross, October 15, 1975.
[74] George Kuyper, "Adventures In Faith," *Southern Workman* (May, 1933). Courtesy of Hampton University Archives
[75] "A Worthwhile Cause," *The Richmond (VA) Times-Dispatch* (September 5, 1933).
[76] I.S. Caldwell, *Bread Cast Upon The Waters Is Returning* (undated). Kautz Family YMCA Archives, University of Minnesota Libraries.
[77] Willie Lee Buffington, *A General Survey of Faith Cabin Library With Its 26 Separate Units (South Carolina)* (June and July, 1940). Courtesy of the South Caroliniana Library, University of South Carolina, Columbia SC.
[78] Rev. John Watson, Letter to Willie Lee Buffington, October 13, 1933. Kautz Family YMCA Archives, University of Minnesota Libraries.
[79] Ibid.
[80] Plumb, "Joy Bells Ringing", 1.
[81] Buffington, *A General Survey of Faith Cabin Library*
[82] Ibid.

Chapter 5
[83] Buffington Interview, 13.
[84] Ibid., 11.
[85] Ibid., 12.
[86] Herman Styler, "Books for the Backwoods," *Together* (April, 1961), 19. Courtesy of the South Caroliniana Library, University of South Carolina, Columbia SC.
[87] Louise Carr, "The Reverend Willie Lee Buffington's Life and Contributions To The Development Of Rural Libraries In The South" (Masters Thesis, Atlanta University). Courtesy of Archives Research Center, Robert W. Woodruff Library, Atlanta University, Atlanta GA.
[88] "Library Founder In Backwoods To Speak Here Friday," *Xenia (OH) Evening Gazette* (August 15, 1936).
[89] Buell, 14.
[90] Catherine Degen, Letter to Willie Lee Buffington, February 19, 1938. Courtesy of the South Caroliniana Library, University of South Carolina, Columbia SC.
[91] Buffington, *A General Survey of Faith Cabin Library,* 13.
[92] Edward Barrett Stanford, *Library Extension Under The Works Progress Administration, Chapter 6* (University of Chicago Press: Chicago, 1941), p.185. Courtesy of the South Caroliniana Library, University of South Carolina, Columbia SC.
[93] Ibid.
[94] Buffington, *A General Survey of Faith Cabin Library,* 16.

[95] Ibid., 21.

[96] Francis W. Allen, "Faith Cabin Libraries," *Library Journal 66* (March 1, 1941, 187-88).

[97] Buffington, *A General Survey of Faith Cabin Library,* 24.

[98] Ibid., 19-20.

[99] Ibid., 26-27.

[100] Styler, *Books for the Backwoods*, 19.

[101] Buffington, *A General Survey of Faith Cabin Library,* 29-30.

[102] Buffington Interview, 12.

[103] Willie Lee Buffington, Letter to Mr. Mendel S. Fletcher, August 10, 1938. Courtesy of Furman University, Alumni Archives, Greenville SC.

[104] Roman Koral, Letter to Willie Lee Buffington, January 12, 1937. Courtesy of the South Caroliniana Library, University of South Carolina, Columbia SC.

Chapter 6

[105] Buffington, *A General Survey of Faith Cabin Library,* 34.

[106] "Enough Books For Two Libraries Given By Elyrians," *The Elyria (OH) Chronicle-Telegram* (November 12, 1938), 2.

[107] *Elyria (OH) Chronicle-Telegram*, September 15, 1939, p.1. Courtesy of the South Caroliniana Library, University of South Carolina, Columbia SC.

[108] Buffington, *A General Survey of Faith Cabin Library,* 34.

[109] Ibid.,36.

[110] Betty Burleigh, "Libraries in Cabins," *World Outlook:General Board of Global Ministries* (March, 1946), 8.

[111] Buffington, *A General Survey of Faith Cabin Library,* 44.

[112] Ibid., 39.

[113] Ibid., 49.

[114] Ibid., 53.

[115] Ibid., 55.

[116] Buffington, Letter to Dr. Channing Tobias, undated. Kautz Family YMCA Archives, University of Minnesota Libraries.

[117] Buffington, *A General Survey of Faith Cabin Library,* 66.

[118] Buffington Interview, 13.

Chapter 7

[119] Buffington, Card to Dr. Channing Tobias, February 17, 1942. Kautz Family YMCA Archives, University of Minnesota Libraries.

[120] Dr. Channing Tobias, Letter to Willie Lee Buffington, February 20, 1942. Kautz Family YMCA Archives, University of Minnesota Libraries.

[121] Buffington, Letter to Dr. Channing Tobias, February 23, 1942. Kautz Family YMCA Archives, University of Minnesota Libraries.

[122] Buffington Interview, 14.

[123] Willie Lee Buffington, Letter to "Dear Faith Cabin Library Friend," October 2, 1942. Kautz Family YMCA Archives, University of Minnesota Libraries.

[124] Buffington, Letter to Dr. Channing Tobias, December 14, 1942. Kautz Family YMCA Archives, University of Minnesota Libraries.

[125] Ibid.

[126] Dr. Channing Tobias, Letter to Willie Lee Buffington, December 16, 1942. Kautz Family YMCA Archives, University of Minnesota Libraries.

[127] Ibid.

[128] Buffington, Letter to Dr. Channing Tobias, December 14, 1942. Kautz Family YMCA Archives, University of Minnesota Libraries.

[129] Anna Murchison, "He Builds Libraries for Negroes," *Southern Baptist Home Missions* (November, 1942). Una R. Lawrence Papers, Southern Baptist Historical Library and Archives, Nashville TN.

[130] Paul C. Carter and Ruth H. Geil, "Faith Cabin Libraries," *Baptist Leader* (November 1943), 2.Courtesy of the South Caroliniana Library, University of South Carolina, Columbia SC.

[131] Stanford, 185.

[132] Willie Lee Buffington, Letter to Una R. Lawrence, August 4, 1944. Una R. Lawrence Papers, Southern Baptist Historical Library and Archives, Nashville TN.

[133] Una R. Lawrence, Letter to Willie Lee Buffington, August 12, 1944. Una R. Lawrence Papers, Southern Baptist Historical Library and Archives, Nashville TN.

[134] Ibid.

[135] Buffington, Letter to Una R. Lawrence, August 20, 1944. Una R. Lawrence Papers, Southern Baptist Historical Library and Archives, Nashville TN.

[136] Ibid.

[137] Ibid.

[138] Lawrence, Letter (fragment) to Willie Lee Buffington, undated. Una R. Lawrence Papers, Southern Baptist Historical Library and Archives, Nashville TN.

[139] Willie Lee Buffington, Letter To Dr. George Nace, April 29, 1950. Courtesy of the South Caroliniana Library, University of South Carolina, Columbia SC.

[140] Paine College Board of Trustee Meeting Minutes, May 24, 1951. Courtesy of Paine College Library, Augusta GA.

[141] Buffington, Letter To Dr. George Nace, April 29, 1950.

[142] Report of Faith Cabin Library Extension of Paine College, To the Board of Trustees, May 25, 1950. Courtesy of Paine College Library, Augusta GA.

[143] Ibid.

[144] Willie Lee Buffington, Letter to Una R. Lawrence, January 9, 1946. Una R. Lawrence Papers, Southern Baptist Historical Library and Archives, Nashville TN.

[145] Ibid.

[146] Burleigh, p.6.

[147] Ibid.

[148] Herman Styler, "He Worked Wonders – With Faith and a Dime," *Coronet* (June, 1947), 47. Courtesy of the South Caroliniana Library, University of South Carolina, Columbia SC.

[149] Willie Lee Buffington, Letter to the New York Conference of Women's Society of Christian Service, October 1, 1947. Courtesy of the South Caroliniana Library, University of South Carolina, Columbia SC.

[150] Jessie Wiley Voils, Letter to Willie Lee Buffington, April 15, 1948. Courtesy of the South Caroliniana Library, University of South Carolina, Columbia SC.

[151] Willie Lee Buffington, Letter (fragment) to Ted Malone, undated. Courtesy of the South Caroliniana Library, University of South Carolina, Columbia SC.

[152] Ted Malone, Broadcast Script of *Westinghouse Presents* (October 6, 1948). Courtesy of the South Caroliniana Library, University of South Carolina, Columbia SC.

[153] Dan Lee, "Faith Cabin Libraries: A Study of an Alternative Library Service in the Segregated South, 1932-1960," *Library History Seminar VIII* (May, 1990), 176. Courtesy of the author.

[154] Estellene Walker, Letter to Willie Lee Buffington, November 15, 1947. Courtesy of the South Caroliniana Library, University of South Carolina, Columbia SC.

[155] Ibid.

[156] Willie Lee Buffington, Letter to Estellene Walker, December 18, 1947. Courtesy of the South Caroliniana Library, University of South Carolina, Columbia SC.

[157] Suzanne O'Donnell, "Equal Opportunities For Both: Julius Rosenwald, Jim Crow, and the Charleston Free Library's Record of Service To Blacks, 1931 To 1960" (Master's Thesis, University of North Carolina, 2000), p.38. Courtesy of the author.

[158] Lee, "Faith Cabin Libraries," 174.

Chapter 8

[159] Benjamin F. Hobert, "Negroes Succeed In Georgia," *Savannah (GA) Morning News* (November 9, 1948).

[160] Willie Lee Buffington, Letter to Mrs. Allen Newkirk, February 23, 1949. Courtesy of the South Caroliniana Library, University of South Carolina, Columbia SC.

[161] Paine College, Report to the Board of Trustees, May 21, 1948. Courtesy of Paine College Library, Augusta GA.

[162] Ibid.

[163] Willie Lee Buffington, Letter to Local Presidents of the Southern Illinois Conference of Women's Society of Christian Service, March, 24, 1949. Courtesy of the South Caroliniana Library, University of South Carolina, Columbia SC.

[164] Buffington, Letter to Mrs. Allen Newkirk.

[165] Willie Lee Buffington, Letter to Genesee New York Conference of Women's Society of Christian Service; November 10, 1948.Courtesy of the South Caroliniana Library, University of South Carolina, Columbia SC.

[166] Buffington, Letter to Local Presidents of the Southern Illinois Conference.

[167] Buffington, Letter to Mrs. Allen Newkirk.

[168] Willie Lee Buffingotn, Letter to North Indiana Conference of Women's Society of Christian Service, April 8, 1949. Courtesy of the South Caroliniana Library, University of South Carolina, Columbia SC.

[169] Ibid.

[170] W.E. West, Letter to Willie Lee Buffington, March 28, 1949. Courtesy of the South Caroliniana Library, University of South Carolina, Columbia SC.

[171] Willie Lee Buffington, Letter to W.D. Tolbert, February 25, 1949. Courtesy of the South Caroliniana Library, University of South Carolina, Columbia SC.

[172] James R. Hightower, Letter to Willie Lee Buffington, November 3, 1949. Courtesy of the South Caroliniana Library, University of South Carolina, Columbia SC.

[173] Willie Lee Buffington, Letter to Mrs. L.T. Clark, March 2, 1949. Courtesy of the South Caroliniana Library, University of South Carolina, Columbia SC.

[174] Earl Brown, Letter to Willie Lee Buffington, December 14, 1948. Courtesy of the South Caroliniana Library, University of South Carolina, Columbia SC.

[175] Earl Brown, Letter to Willie Lee Buffington, December 22, 1948. Courtesy of the South Caroliniana Library, University of South Carolina, Columbia SC.

[176] Susan Schramm-Pate and Rhonda Jeffries, Grappling With Diversity: Readings on Civil Rights Pedagogy and Critical Multiculturalism, Chapter 4 (Albany NY: State University of New York Press, 2008), p.91.

[177] Louise Bennett, Letter to Willie Lee Buffington, January 31, 1950. Courtesy of the South Caroliniana Library, University of South Carolina, Columbia SC.

[178] Buffington, Letter to Dr. George Nace, April 29, 1950.

[179] Don F. Pielstick, Letter to Willie Lee Buffington, May 4, 1950. Courtesy of the South Caroliniana Library, University of South Carolina, Columbia SC.

[180] Willie Lee Buffington, Letter to Dr. W.F. Quillian, May 11, 1950. Courtesy of the South Caroliniana Library, University of South Carolina, Columbia SC.

[181] Willie Lee Buffington, Letter to Dr. Edward G. Mackey, May 11, 1950. Courtesy of the South Caroliniana Library, University of South Carolina, Columbia SC.

[182] Willie Lee Buffington, Letter to Louise Bennett, May 22, 1950. Courtesy of the South Caroliniana Library, University of South Carolina, Columbia SC.

Chapter 9

[183] Paine College, Report of Faith Cabin Library Extension: To the Board of Trustees, May 25, 1950. Courtesy of Paine College Library, Augusta GA.

[184] Ibid.

[185] Ibid.

[186] Ibid.

[187] Ibid.

[188] Ibid.

[189] Ibid.

[190] Henry Sprinkle, "The Miracle of the Books," *World Outlook: General Board of Global Ministrie* (September, 1950), p.3. Courtesy of the South Caroliniana Library, University of South Carolina, Columbia SC.

[191] Willie Lee Buffington, Letter fragment to Dr. Edgar Love, November 13, 1950. Courtesy of the South Caroliniana Library, University of South Carolina, Columbia SC.

[192] Ibid.

[193] Buffington, Letter to Dr.DonPielstick, November 13, 1950.

[194] Dr. Maurice Cherry Telephone Interview, January 6, 2011.

[195] Batten, Barton, Durstine& Osborne, Letter to Willie Lee Buffington, February 28, 1951. Courtesy of the South Caroliniana Library, University of South Carolina, Columbia SC.

[196] Robert Cummings, Letter to Willie Lee Buffington, April 17, 1951. Courtesy of the South Caroliniana Library, University of South Carolina, Columbia SC.

[197] Cherry Interview.

[198] Dr. B.E. Geer, letter to Willie Lee Buffington, March 14, 1951. Courtesy of the South Caroliniana Library, University of South Carolina, Columbia SC.

[199] Cherry Interview.

[200] Ibid.

[201] Ibid.

[202] Ibid.

[203] Paine College, Board of Trustee Meeting Minutes, May 24, 1951. Courtesy of Paine College Library, Augusta GA.

[204] Ibid.

[205] Ibid.

[206] Ibid.

[207] Ibid.

[208] Paine College, Committee on Faith Cabin Library Report to the Board of Trustees, May 25, 1951. Courtesy of Paine College Library, Augusta GA.

[209] Willie Lee Buffington, Letter to Mrs. B.E. Mayes. Courtesy of the South Caroliniana Library, University of South Carolina, Columbia SC.

[210] Carol Murray, "Danville Woman Gives Away Books," Danville (IL) Commercial News (September 2, 1951).

Chapter 10

[211] Lee, "Faith Cabin Libraries," 177.

[212] Neal, "The Bookshelves Filled By Faith."

[213] Paine College, Faith Cabin Library Report to the Student-Faculty Assembly, October 2, 1951. Courtesy of Paine College Library, Augusta GA.

[214] Report of Faith Cabin Library Extension of Paine College: To the Executive Committee of Board of Trustees, October 4, 1951. Courtesy of Paine College Library, Augusta GA.

[215] Annual Report, Faith Cabin Library Extension of Paine College: To the Board of Trustees, 1951-52. Courtesy of Paine College Library, Augusta GA.

[216] Ibid.

[217] Ibid.

[218] Ibid.

[219] Ibid.

[220] Annual Report, Faith Cabin Library Extension of Paine College: To the Board of Trustees, 1952-53. Courtesy of Paine College Library, Augusta GA.

[221] Ibid.

[222] Ibid.

[223] *Red Bank (NJ) Register*, March 18, 1954.

[224] Willie Lee Buffington, "The Ministry of Books," *World Outlook:General Board of Global Ministries* (January 1955). Courtesy of the South Caroliniana Library, University of South Carolina, Columbia SC.

[225] A.H. King, Letter to Willie Lee Buffington, May 2, 1956. Courtesy of the South Caroliniana Library, University of South Carolina, Columbia SC.

[226] Annual Report, Faith Cabin Library Extension of Paine College: To the Board of Trustees, 1956-57. Courtesy of Paine College Library, Augusta GA.

[227] Willie Lee Buffington, Letter to Robert Lester, September 30, 1956. Courtesy of the South Caroliniana Library, University of South Carolina, Columbia SC.

[228] Annual Report, Faith Cabin Library Extension, 1956-57.

[229] Ibid.

[230] Erma Cameron and Daniel T. Grant, Letter to Willie Lee Buffington, March 11, 1957. Courtesy of the South Caroliniana Library, University of South Carolina, Columbia SC.

[231] Robert L. Cousins, Letter to Willie Lee Buffington, October 10, 1957. Courtesy of the South Caroliniana Library, University of South Carolina, Columbia SC.

[232] Robert L. Cousins, Letter to D.F.Osborne, November 14, 1957. Courtesy of the South Caroliniana Library, University of South Carolina, Columbia SC.

[233] Annual Report, Faith Cabin Library Extension, 1956-57.

[234] Ibid.

[235] 1958 Lane Bryant Annual Awards Ceremony Program. Courtesy of Paine College Library, Augusta GA.

[236] "Augustan, Founder of Library Chain for Negroes, Receives $1,000 Award," *Augusta (GA) Herald* (November 13, 1958).

[237] Willie Lee Buffington, Letter to Gwendolyn Ross, January 13, 1975. Courtesy of the South Caroliniana Library, University of South Carolina, Columbia SC.

Chapter 11

[238] Beatrice Plumb, "A Dream, a Dime – and Faith," from *Lives That Inspire* (T.S. Denison: Minneapolis MN, 1962), p.27.

[239] Mary Parkman Interview, April 11, 2010.

[240] Dr. Marcus Clayton Interview, January 2, 2011.
[241] "175 lbs. of new and used books have been sent to Faith Cabin Library," *Emporia (KS) Gazette*, February 12, 1962.
[242] Paine College, Board of Trustees Meeting Minutes, April 1-2, 1963.
[243] Daytona Beach (FL) *Morning Journal*, April 11, 1964.
[244] Silas Norman Jr., MD E-mail Interview, January 26, 2011.
[245] Ibid.
[246] Buell, p.5
[247] Norman Interview.
[248] Cherry Interview.
[249] Paine College, Board of Trustees Meeting Minutes, May 20, 1960. Courtesy of Paine College Library, Augusta GA.
[250] Cherry Interview.
[251] Report of Faith Cabin Library Extension of Paine College: To the Executive Committee of Board of Trustees, February 10, 1966. Courtesy of Paine College Library, Augusta GA.
[252] Ibid.
[253] Paine College, Board of Trustees Meeting Minutes, May 7-8, 1965. Courtesy of Paine College Library, Augusta GA.
[254] Report of Faith Cabin Library Extension of Paine College, February 10, 1966. Courtesy of Paine College Library, Augusta GA.
[255] Lee, "Faith Cabin Libraries," 180.
[256] Report of Faith Cabin Library Extension of Paine College, February 10, 1966.
[257] Ibid.
[258] Ibid.
[259] Paine College, Board of Trustees Meeting Minutes, April 26, 1969. Courtesy of Paine College Library, Augusta GA.
[260] Buffington, *A General Survey of Faith Cabin Library*, 11.

Chapter 12
[261] Buffington, Letter to Gwendolyn Ross, January 13, 1975.
[262] Ibid.
[263] Cherry Interview.
[264] Buffington, Letter to Gwendolyn Ross.
[265] Report of Faith Cabin Library Extension of Paine College: To the Executive Committee of Board of Trustees, April 25, 1970.
[266] Dr. Arthur Holt Interview, June 11, 2010.
[267] Ibid.
[268] Ibid.
[269] Dr. Arthur Holt, *The 5K Buffet*, Sermon at Memorial United Methodist Church, August 3, 2008.
[270] Dr. Arthur Holt, E-mail Interview, April 26, 2010.
[271] Dr. Arthur Holt, E-mail Interview, September 7, 2012.
[272] Holt Interview, June 11, 2010.

[273] Ibid.

[274] Buffington Interview.

[275] Ibid.

[276] Parkman Interview.

[277] Holt Interview, June 11, 2010.

[278] Mary Parkman, "The Reverend Willie Lee Buffington," from Our Saluda County Ancestors (Saluda SC, 2010), p.10.

[279] Holt E-mail interview, April 26, 2010.

[280] Holt Interview, June 11, 2010.

[281] Holt, *The 5K Buffet*, August 3, 2008.

[282] Willie Lee Buffington, Sermon at Tignall United Methodist Church, Tignall GA, March 24, 1971.

[283] Carr, p.44.

[284] Ibid., 51.

[285] Tobias, Letter to Willie Lee Buffington, undated. Kautz Family YMCA Archives, University of Minnestoa Libraries.

[286] Carr, p.42.

[287] Dr. Robert Williams Interview, June 2010.

[288] Tobias, Letter to Willie Lee Buffington, undated. Kautz Family YMCA Archives, University of Minnesota Libraries.

[289] Carr, p.43.

[290] Ibid., 44.

[291] Tobias, Letter to Willie Lee Buffington, undated. Kautz Family YMCA Archives, University of Minnesota Libraries.

[292] Ibid.

[293] Carr, p.43.

[294] Ibid.,42.

About The Author

Thomas K. Perry earned a BA (1974) and MA (1977) from Wake Forest University. He is the author of *Textile League Baseball* (1993); *Shoeless Joe*, a play about Joe Jackson (1995); co-author of *The Southern Textile Basketball Tournament* (1997); and *Just Joe: Baseball's Natural, as told by his wife* (2007), his first novel. He lives in Newberry SC.

Made in the USA
Lexington, KY
10 July 2017